Ninja Foodi Grill Cookbook 2021

Easy, Quick & Delicious Recipes for Indoor Grilling and Air Frying Perfection

(for Beginners and Advanced Users)

Cecilia Hobbs

Table of Contents

Introduction

The Ninja Foodi 5-in-1 Indoor Grill is an incredible multi-purpose cooking machine. It can air fry, roast, bake, dehydrate and grill indoors. It won't do your laundry or wash your car, but it does seem to do everything else. Meats, vegetables, and even fruit come out with juicy perfection. You can also use the Ninja Foodi 5-in-1 Indoor Grill to make dried fruit and beef jerky snacks.

The features of Ninja Foodi Grill

• The Ninja Foodi Pro Grill with Integrated Smart Probe. The grill that sears, sizzles, and air fry crisps. Indoor grill and air fryer
• Confidently cook food on the inside using the integrated Smart Probe and char-grill every side with superhot Cyclonic Grilling Technology. 500F air circulates around food for amazing Surround Searing, while the 500F high-density grill grate creates char-grilled marks and flavors
• Perfect char-grilled results with GrillControl settings: Low, Medium, High, and Max. The wide temperature range of 105F500F and variable fan speed enable 5 fast, versatile cooking functions: Grill, Air Crisp, Dehydrate, Roast, and Bake
• Air fry crisp with up to 75% less fat than deep frying (tested against hand-cut, deep-fried French fries), using the included 4-qt crisper basket
• No need to cut into foods or constantly probe them like when using an instant read thermometer. Eliminate guesswork and never worry about under or overcooking with the Integrated Smart Probe. Multi-task with peace of mind as food cooks to perfection
• Intuitive digital display lets you easily choose a cooking function and see your food's internal temperature as the Integrated Smart Probe monitors it. The grill will conveniently alert you when your food is perfectly cooked
• Virtually smoke free with unique Smoke Control Technology. The combination of a temperature-controlled grill grate, splatter shield, and cool-air zone reduces smoke, keeping it out of the kitchen

Tips for use Ninja Foodi Grill

When you are cooking for the first time with your Foodi grill, you must first wash the detachable cooking parts with warm soapy water to remove any oil and debris. Let them air dry and place them back inside once you are ready to cook. An easy-to-follow instruction guide comes with each unit, so make sure to go over it before cooking.

Position your grill on a level and secure surface. Leave at least 6 inches of space around it, especially at the back where the air intake vent and air socket are located. Ensure that the splatter guard is installed whenever the grill is in use. This is a wire mesh that covers the heating element on the inside of the lid.

1. Grilling. Plug your unit into an outlet and power on the grill. Use the grill grate over the cooking pot and choose the grill function. This has four default temperature settings of low at 400 degrees F, medium at 450 degrees F, high at 500 degrees F, and max at 510 degrees F. Set the time needed to cook. You may check the grilling cheat sheet that comes with your unit to guide you with the time and temperature settings. It is best to check the food regularly depending on the doneness you prefer and to avoid overcooking. Once the required settings are selected, press start and wait for the digital display to show 'add food'. The unit will start to preheat similar to an oven and will show the progress through the display. This step takes about 8 minutes. If you need to check the food or flip it, the timer will pause and resume once the lid is closed. The screen will show 'Done' once the timer and cooking have been completed. Power off the unit and unplug the device. Leave the hood open to let the unit cool faster.

2. Bake. Remove the grates and use the cooking pot. Choose the bake setting and set your preferred temperature and time. Preheating will take about 3 minutes. Once done with preheating, you may put the ingredients directly on the cooking pot, or you may use your regular baking tray. An 8-inch baking tray can fit inside as well as similar-sized oven-safe containers.

3. Roasting. Remove the grill grates and use the cooking pot that comes with the unit. You may also purchase their roasting rack for this purpose.

Press the roast option and set the timer between 1 to 4 hours depending on the recipe requirements. The Foodi will preheat for 3 minutes regardless of the time you have set.

Once ready, place the meat directly on the roasting pot or rack.

Check occasionally for doneness. A meat thermometer is another useful tool to get your meats perfectly cooked.

4. Air crisping. Put the crisper basket in and close the lid. Press the air crisp option then the start button. The default temperature is set at 390° F and will preheat at about 3 minutes. You can adjust the temperature and time by pressing the buttons beside these options.

If you do not need to preheat, just press the air crisp button a second time and the display will show you the 'add food' message. Put the food inside and shake or turn every 10 minutes. Use oven mitts or tongs with silicone when doing this.

5. Dehydrating. Place the first layer of food directly on the cooking pot. Add the crisper basket and add one more layer. Choose the dehydrate setting and set the timer between 7 to 10 hours. You may check the progress from time to time.

6.Cooking frozen foods. Choose the medium heat, which is 450° F using the grill option. You may also use the air crisp option if you are cooking fries, vegetables, and other frozen foods. Set the time needed for your recipe. Add a few minutes to compensate for the thawing.

Flip or shake after a few minutes to cook the food evenly.

Amazing Breakfast Recipes

Hearty Ninja Food Bean

Prepping time: 5 minutes

Cooking time: 10 minutes

Servings: 4

Ingredients

- Fresh ground black pepper
- Flaky sea salt
- Pinch of pepper
- 1 lemon, juiced
- 2 tablespoon oil
- 1-pound green bean, trimmed

Directions

1. Take a medium bowl and add the green bean
2. Mix and stir well
3. Preheat your Ninja Foodi Grill to MAX and set the timer to 10 minutes
4. Wait until you hear a beep
5. Transfer beans to the grill grate, cook for 8-10 minutes
6. Toss well to ensure that all sides cooked evenly
7. Squeeze a bit of lemon juice on top
8. Season with salt, pepper and pepper flakes according to your taste
9. Enjoy!

Nutritional Values (Per Serving)

Calories: 100, Fat: 7 g, Saturated Fat: 1 g, Carbohydrates: 10 g, Fiber: 4 g, Sodium: 30 mg, Protein: 2 g

Early Morning Kale and Sausage Delight

Prepping time: 10 minutes

Cooking time: 10 minutes

Servings: 4

Ingredients

- Olive oil as needed
- 1 cup mushrooms
- 2 cups kale,e chopped
- 4 sausage links
- 4 medium eggs
- 1 medium yellow onion, sweet

Directions

1. Open the lid of your Ninja Foodi Grill and arrange the Grill Grate
2. Pre-heat your Ninja Foodi Grill to HIGH and set the timer to 5 minutes
3. Once you hear the beeping sound, arrange sausages over the grill grate
4. Cook for 2 minutes, flip and cook for 3 minutes more
5. Take a baking pan and spread out the kale, onion, mushroom, sausage and crack an egg on top
6. Cook on BAKE mode on 350 degrees F for about 5 minutes more
7. Serve and enjoy!

Nutritional Values (Per Serving)

Calories: 236, Fat: 12 g, Saturated Fat: 2 g, Carbohydrates: 17 g, Fiber: 4 g, Sodium: 369 mg, Protein: 18 g

Energetic Bagel Platter

Prepping time: 5-10 minutes

Cooking time: 8 minutes

Servings: 4

Ingredients

- 4 bagels, halved
- 2 tablespoons coconut flakes
- 1 cup fine sugar
- 2 tablespoons black coffee, prepared and cooled down
- ¼ cup of coconut milk

Directions

1. Take your Ninja Foodi Grill and open the lid
2. Arrange grill grate and close top
3. Pre-heat Ninja Foodi by pressing the "GRILL" option and setting it to "MEDIUM."
4. Set the timer to 8 minutes
5. Let it pre-heat until you hear a beep
6. Arrange bagels over grill grate and lock lid
7. Cook for 2 minutes
8. Flip sausages and cook for 2 minutes more
9. Repeat the same procedure to Grill remaining Bagels
10. Take a mixing bowl and mix the remaining ingredients
11. Pour the sauce over grilled bagels
12. Serve and enjoy!

Nutrition Values (Per Serving)

Calories: 300, Fat: 23 g, Saturated Fat: 12 g, Carbohydrates: 42 g, Fiber: 4 g, Sodium: 340 mg, Protein: 18 g

Juicy Stuffed Bell Peppers

Prepping time: 10 minutes

Cooking time: 15 minutes

Servings: 4

Ingredients

- 4 slices bacon, cooked and chopped
- 4 large eggs
- 1 cup cheddar cheese, shredded
- 4 bell peppers, seeded and tops removed
- Chopped parsley for garnish
- Salt and pepper to taste

Directions

1. Divide cheese and bacon equally and stuff into your bell pepper
2. Add eggs into each bell pepper
3. Season with salt and pepper
4. Pre-heat your Ninja Foodi by pressing the "AIR CRISP" option and setting it to "390 Degrees F."
5. Set the timer to 15 minutes
6. Let it pre-heat until you hear a beep
7. Transfer bell pepper to your cooking basket and transfer to Ninja Foodi Grill
8. Lock lid and cook for 10-15 minutes
9. Cook until egg whites are cooked well until the yolks are slightly runny
10. Remove peppers from the basket and garnish with parsley
11. Serve and enjoy!

Nutrition Values (Per Serving)

Calories: 326, Fat: 23 g, Saturated Fat: 10 g, Carbohydrates: 10 g, Fiber: 2 g, Sodium: 781 mg, Protein: 22 g

Butternut Squash with Italian Herbs

Prepping time: 5-10 minutes

Cooking time: 16 minutes

Servings: 4

Ingredients

- 1 medium butternut squash, peeled, seeded, and cut into ½ inch slices
- 1 teaspoon dried thyme
- 1 tablespoon olive oil
- 1 and ½ teaspoons oregano, dried
- ¼ teaspoon black pepper
- ½ teaspoon salt

Directions

1. Add all the ingredients into a mixing bowl and mix it
2. Pre-heat your Ninja Foodi by pressing the "GRILL" option and setting it to "MED."
3. Set the timer to 16 minutes
4. Allow it to pre-heat until you hear a beep
5. Arrange squash slices over the grill grate
6. Cook for 8 minutes
7. Flip them and cook for 8 minutes more
8. Serve and enjoy!

Nutrition Values (Per Serving)

Calories: 238, Fat: 12 g, Saturated Fat: 2 g, Carbohydrates: 36 g, Fiber: 3 g, Sodium: 128 mg, Protein: 15 g

Mushroom Pepper Meal

Prepping time: 10 minutes

Cooking time:10 minutes

Servings: 4

Ingredients

- 4 cremini mushrooms, sliced
- 4 large eggs
- ½ cup cheddar cheese, shredded
- ½ onion, chopped
- ¼ cup whole milk
- Sea salt
- ½ bell pepper, seeded and diced
- Black pepper

Directions

1. Add eggs and milk into a medium bowl
2. Whisk them together
3. Add mushrooms, onion, bell pepper, and cheese
4. Mix them well
5. Preheat by selecting the "BAKE" option and setting it to 400 degrees F
6. Set the timer for 10 minutes
7. Pour the egg mixture into the baking pan and spread evenly
8. Let it pre-heat until you hear a beep
9. Then close the lid
10. Cook for 10 minutes
11. Serve and enjoy!

Nutrition Values (Per Serving)

Calories: 153, Fat: 10 g, Saturated Fat: 2 g, Carbohydrates: 5 g, Fiber: 1 g, Sodium: 494 mg, Protein: 11 g

Completely Stuffed Up Bacon and Pepper

Prepping time: 10 minutes

Cooking time: 15 minutes

Servings: 4

Ingredients

- Chopped parsley, for garnish
- Salt and pepper to taste
- 4 whole large eggs
- 4 bell pepper, seeded and tops removed
- 4 slices bacon, cooked and chopped
- 1 cup cheddar cheese, shredded

Directions

1. Take the bell pepper and divide the cheese and bacon evenly between them
2. Crack eggs into each of the bell pepper
3. Season the bell pepper with salt and pepper
4. Pre-heat your Ninja Food Grill in AIR CRISP mode with temperature to 390 degrees F
5. Set timer to 15 minutes
6. Once you hear the beep, transfer the bell pepper to cooking basket
7. Transfer your prepared pepper to Ninja Foodi Grill and cook for 10-15 minutes until the eggs are cooked, and the yolks are just slightly runny
8. Garnish with a bit of parsley
9. Enjoy!

Nutritional Values (Per Serving)

Calories: 326, Fat: 23 g, Saturated Fat: 10 g, Carbohydrates: 10 g, Fiber: 2 g, Sodium: 781 mg, Protein: 22 g

Epic Breakfast Burrito

Prepping time: 5-10 minutes

Cooking time: 30 minutes

Servings: 4

Ingredients

- 12 tortillas
- Salt and pepper to taste
- 2 cups potatoes, diced
- 3 cups cheddar cheese, shredded
- 10 whole eggs, beaten
- 1 pound breakfast sausage
- 1 teaspoon olive oil

Directions

1. Pour olive oil into a pan over medium heat.
2. Cook potatoes and sausage for 7 to 10 minutes, stirring frequently.
3. Spread this mixture on the bottom of the Ninja Foodi Grill pot.
4. Season with salt and pepper.
5. Pour the eggs and cheese on top.
6. Select bake setting.
7. Cook at 325 degrees F for 20 minutes.
8. Top the tortilla with the cooked mixture and roll.
9. Sprinkle cheese on the top side.
10. Add Crisper basket to Ninja Foodi Grill
11. AIR CRISP the Burritos for 10 minutes at 375 degrees F
12. Serve and enjoy!

Nutrition Values (Per Serving)

Calories: 400, Fat: 20 g, Saturated Fat: 10 g, Carbohydrates: 36 g, Fiber: 5 g, Sodium: 675 mg, Protein: 22 g

Simple Zucchini Egg Muffins

Prepping time: 5-10 minutes

Cooking time: 7 minutes

Servings: 4

Ingredients

- 4 whole eggs
- 2 tablespoons almond flour
- 1 zucchini, grated
- 1 teaspoon butter
- ½ teaspoon salt

Directions

1. Take a small-sized bowl and add almond flour, salt, zucchini. Mix well

2. Take muffin molds and grease them gently, add the zucchini mix

3. Arrange your molds in Ninja Foodi Grill and cook on "AIR CRISP" mode for 7 minutes at a temperature of 375 degrees F

4. Serve and enjoy the meal once complete!

Nutritional Values (Per Serving)

Calories: 94, Fat: 8 g, Saturated Fat: 1.5 g, Carbohydrates: 2 g, Fiber: 0.5 g, Sodium: 209 mg, Protein: 7 g

The Broccoli and Maple Mix

Prepping time: 5-10 minutes

Cooking time:10 minutes

Servings: 4

Ingredients

- 2 heads broccoli, cut into florets
- 4 tablespoons soy sauce
- 2 teaspoons maple syrup
- 4 tablespoon balsamic vinegar
- 2 tablespoons canola oil
- Red pepper flakes and sesame seeds for garnish

Directions

1. Take a shallow mixing bowl and add vinegar, soy sauce, oil, maple syrup
2. Whisk the whole mixture thoroughly
3. Add broccoli to the mix
4. Keep it aside
5. Set your Ninja Foodi Grill to "MAX" mode
6. Set the timer to 10 minutes
7. Once you hear the beep, add prepared broccoli over Grill Grate
8. Cook for 10 minutes
9. Top with sesame seeds, pepper flakes
10. Serve and enjoy!

Nutrition Values (Per Serving)

Calories: 141, Fat: 7 g, Saturated Fat: 1 g, Carbohydrates: 14 g, Fiber: 4 g, Sodium: 853 mg, Protein: 4 g

Early Morning Frittata

Prepping time: 10 minutes

Cooking time:10 minutes

Servings: 4

Ingredients

- 4 large eggs
- 4 cremini mushrooms, sliced
- ½ bell pepper, seeded and diced
- ½ cup shredded cheddar cheese
- ½ onion, chopped
- ¼ cup whole milk
- Salt and pepper to taste

Directions

1. Add eggs and milk into a medium-sized bowl
2. Whisk it and then season with salt and pepper
3. Then add bell pepper, onion, mushroom, cheese
4. Mix them well
5. Pre-heat Ninja Foodi by pressing the "BAKE" option and setting it to "400 Degrees F."
6. Set the timer to 10 minutes
7. Let it pre-heat until you hear a beep
8. Pour Egg Mixture in your Ninja Foodi Bake Pan, spread well
9. Transfer to Grill and lock lid
10. Bake for 10 minutes until lightly golden
11. Serve and enjoy!

Nutrition Values (Per Serving)

Calories: 153, Fat: 10 g, Saturated Fat: 5 g, Carbohydrates: 5 g, Fiber: 1 g, Sodium: 177 mg, Protein: 11 g

Refreshing Chicken and Poultry Recipes

Moroccan Roast Chicken

Prepping time: 5-10 minutes

Cooking time: 22 minutes

Servings: 4

Ingredients

- 3 tablespoons plain yogurt
- 4 skinless, boneless chicken thighs
- 4 garlic cloves, chopped
- ½ teaspoon salt
- 1/3 cup olive oil
- ½ teaspoon fresh flat-leaf parsley, chopped
- 2 teaspoons ground cumin
- 2 teaspoons paprika
- ¼ teaspoon crushed red pepper flakes

Directions

1. Take your food processor and add garlic, yogurt, salt, oil and blend well

2. Take a mixing bowl and add chicken, red pepper flakes, paprika, cumin, parsley, garlic, and mix well

3. Let it marinate for 2-4 hours

4. Pre-heat Ninja Foodi by pressing the "ROAST" option and setting it to "400 degrees F" and timer to 23 minutes

5. Let it pre-heat until you hear a beep

6. Arrange chicken directly inside your cooking pot and lock lid, cook for 15 minutes, flip and cook for the remaining time

7. Serve and enjoy with yogurt dip!

Nutrition Values (Per Serving)

Calories: 321, Fat: 24 g, Saturated Fat: 5 g, Carbohydrates: 6 g, Fiber: 2 g, Sodium: 602 mg, Protein: 21 g

Grilled BBQ Turkey

Prepping time: 5-10 min.

Cooking time: 30 min.

Servings: 5-6

Ingredients

- 1/2 cup minced parsley
- 1/2 cup chopped green onions
- 4 garlic cloves, minced
- 1 cup Greek yogurt
- 1/2 cup lemon juice
- 1 teaspoon dried rosemary, crushed
- 1/3 cup canola oil
- 4 tablespoons minced dill
- 1 teaspoon salt
- 1/2 teaspoon pepper
- 1-3 pound turkey breast half, bone in

Directions

1. In a mixing bowl, combine all the ingredients except the turkey. Add and coat the turkey evenly. Refrigerate for 8 hours to marinate.

2. Take Ninja Foodi Grill, arrange it over your kitchen platform, and open the top lid.

3. Arrange the grill grate and close the top lid.

4. Press "GRILL" and select the "HIGH" grill function. Adjust the timer to 30 minutes and then press "START/STOP." Ninja Foodi will start pre-heating.

5. Ninja Foodi is preheated and ready to cook when it starts to beep. After you hear a beep, open the top lid.

6. Arrange the turkey over the grill grate.

7. Close the top lid and cook for 15 minutes. Now open the top lid, flip the turkey.

8. Close the top lid and cook for 15 more minutes. Cook until the food thermometer reaches 350°F.

9. Slice and serve.

Nutrition Values (Per Serving)

Calories: 426, Fat: 8.5g, Saturated Fat: 2g, Trans Fat: 0g, Carbohydrates: 22g, Fiber: 3g, Sodium: 594mg, Protein: 38g

Sweet and Sour Chicken BBQ

Prepping time: 10 minutes

Cooking time: 40 minutes

Servings: 4

Ingredients

- 6 chicken drumsticks
- ¾ cup of sugar
- 1 cup of soy sauce
- 1 cup of water
- ¼ cup garlic, minced
- ¼ cup tomato paste
- ¾ cup onion, minced
- 1 cup white vinegar
- Salt and pepper, to taste

Directions

1. Take a Ziploc bag and add all ingredients into it
2. Marinate for at least 2 hours in your refrigerator
3. Insert the crisper basket, and close the hood
4. Pre-heat Ninja Foodi by squeezing the "AIR CRISP" alternative at 390 degrees F for 40 minutes
5. Place the grill pan accessory in the Grill
6. Flip the chicken after every 10 minutes
7. Take a saucepan and pour the marinade into it and heat over medium flame until sauce thickens
8. Brush with the glaze
9. Serve warm and enjoy!

Nutrition Values (Per Serving)

Calories: 460, Fat: 20 g, Saturated Fat: 5 g, Carbohydrates: 26 g, Fiber: 3 g, Sodium: 126 mg, Protein: 28 g

Alfredo Chicken Apples

Prepping time: 5-10 minutes

Cooking time: 20 minutes

Servings: 4

Ingredients

- 1 large apple, wedged
- 1 tablespoon lemon juice
- 4 chicken breasts, halved
- 4 teaspoon chicken seasoning
- 4 slices provolone cheese
- ¼ cup blue cheese, crumbled
- ½ cup alfredo sauce

Directions

1. Take a bowl and add chicken, season it well
2. Take another bowl and add in apple, lemon juice
3. Pre-heat Ninja Foodi by pressing the "GRILL" option and setting it to "MED" and timer to 20 minutes
4. Let it pre-heat until you hear a beep
5. Arrange chicken over Grill Grate, lock lid and cook for 8 minutes, flip and cook for 8 minutes more
6. Grill apple in the same manner for 2 minutes per side (making sure to remove chicken beforehand)
7. Serve chicken with pepper, apple, blue cheese, and alfredo sauce
8. Enjoy!

Nutrition Values (Per Serving)

Calories: 247, Fat: 19 g, Saturated Fat: 6 g, Carbohydrates: 29 g, Fiber: 6 g, Sodium: 853 mg, Protein: 14 g

The Tarragon Chicken Meal

Prepping time: 10 minutes, Cooking time: 5 minutes, Servings: 4

Ingredients

For Chicken

- 1 and ½ pounds chicken tenders
- Salt as needed
- 3 tablespoons tarragon leaves, chopped
- 1 teaspoon lemon zest, grated
- 2 tablespoons fresh lemon juice
- 2 tablespoons extra virgin olive oil

For Sauce

- 2 tablespoons fresh lemon juice
- 2 tablespoons butter, salted
- ½ cup heavy whip cream

Directions

1. Prepare your chicken by taking a baking dish and arranging the chicken over the dish in a single layer

2. Season generously with salt and pepper

3. Sprinkle chopped tarragon and lemon zest all around the tenders

4. Drizzle lemon juice and olive oil on top

5. Let them sit for 10 minutes

6. Drain them well

7. Insert Grill Grate in your Ninja Foodi Grill and set to HIGH temperature

8. Set timer to 4 minutes

9. Once you hear the beep, place chicken tenders in your grill grate

10. Let it cook for 3-4 minutes until cooked completely

11. Do in batches if needed

12. Transfer the cooked chicken tenders to a platter

13. For the sauce, take a small-sized saucepan

14. Add cream, butter and lemon juice and bring to a boil

15. Once thickened enough, pour the mix over chicken

16. Serve and enjoy!

17. Serve and enjoy once ready!

Nutrition Values (Per Serving)

Calories: 263, Fat: 18 g, Saturated Fat: 4 g, Carbohydrates: 7 g, Fiber: 1 g, Sodium: 363 mg, Protein: 19 g

Hearty Chicken Zucchini Kabobs

Prepping time: 10 minutes

Cooking time: 15 minutes

Servings: 4

Ingredients

- 1-pound chicken breast, boneless, skinless and cut into cubes of 2 inches
- 2 tablespoons Greek yogurt, plain
- 4 lemons juice
- 1 lemon zest
- ¼ cup extra-virgin olive oil
- 2 tablespoons oregano
- 1 red onion, quartered
- 1 zucchini, sliced
- 4 garlic cloves, minced
- 1 teaspoon of sea salt
- ½ teaspoon ground black pepper

Directions

1. Take a mixing bowl, add the Greek yogurt, lemon juice, oregano, garlic, zest, salt, and pepper, combine them well
2. Add the chicken and coat well, refrigerate for 1-2 hours to marinate
3. Arrange the grill grate and close the lid
4. Pre-heat Ninja Foodi by pressing the "GRILL" option and setting it to "MED" and timer to 7 minutes
5. Take the skewers, thread the chicken, zucchini and red onion and thread alternatively
6. Let it pre-heat until you hear a beep
7. Arrange the skewers over the grill grate lock lid and cook until the timer reads zero
8. Baste the kebabs with a marinating mixture in between
9. Take out your when it reaches 165 degrees F
10. Serve warm and enjoy!

Nutrition Values (Per Serving)

Calories: 277, Fat: 15 g, Saturated Fat: 4 g, Carbohydrates: 10 g, Fiber: 2 g, Sodium: 146 mg

Daisy Fresh Maple Chicken

Prepping time: 10 minutes

Cooking time: 15 minutes

Servings: 4

Ingredients

- 2 teaspoons onion powder
- 2 teaspoons garlic powder
- 3 garlic cloves, minced
- 1/3 cup soy sauce
- 1 cup maple syrup
- ¼ cup teriyaki sauce
- 1 teaspoon black pepper
- 2 pounds chicken wings, bone-in

Directions

1. Take a medium-sized bowl and add soy sauce, garlic, pepper, maple syrup, garlic powder, onion powder, teriyaki sauce and mix well

2. Add the chicken wings to the mixture and coat it gently

3. Preheat your Ninja Foodi Grill in MED mode, setting the timer to 10 minutes

4. Once you hear a beep, arrange your prepared wings in the grill grate

5. Cook for 5 minutes, flip and cook for 5 minutes more until the internal temperature reaches 165 degrees F

6. Serve!

Nutrition Values (Per Serving)

Calories: 543, Fat: 26 g, Saturated Fat: 6 g, Carbohydrates: 46 g, Fiber: 4 g, Sodium: 648 mg, Protein: 42 g

Chicken Chili and Beans

Prepping time: 10 minutes

Cooking time: 15 minutes

Servings: 4

Ingredients

- 1 and ¼ pounds chicken breast, cut into pieces
- 1 can corn
- ¼ teaspoon garlic powder
- 1 can black beans, drained and rinsed
- 1 tablespoon oil
- 2 tablespoons chili powder
- 1 bell pepper, chopped
- ¼ teaspoon garlic powder
- ¼ teaspoon salt

Directions

1. Pre-heat Ninja Foodi by squeezing the "AIR CRISP" alternative and setting it to "360 Degrees F" and timer to 15 minutes

2. Place all the ingredients in your Ninja Foodi Grill cooking basket/alternatively, you may use a dish to mix the ingredients and then put the dish in the cooking basket

3. Stir to mix well

4. Cook for 15 minutes

5. Serve and enjoy!

Nutrition Values (Per Serving)

Calories: 220, Fat: 4 g, Saturated Fat: 1 g, Carbohydrates: 24 g, Fiber: 2 g, Sodium: 856 mg, Protein: 20 g

Chicken Zucchini Kebabs

Prepping time: 5-10 minutes

Cooking time: 15 minutes

Servings: 4

Ingredients

- Juice of 4 lemons
- Grated zest of 1 lemon
- 1-pound boneless, skinless chicken breasts, cut into cubes of 2 inches
- 2 tablespoons plain Greek yogurt
- ¼ cup extra-virgin olive oil
- 4 garlic cloves, minced
- 1 teaspoon sea salt
- ½ teaspoon ground black pepper
- 2 tablespoons dried oregano
- 1 red onion, quartered
- 1 zucchini, sliced

Directions

1. In a mixing bowl, add the Greek yogurt, oil, lemon juice, zest, garlic, oregano, salt, and pepper. Combine the ingredients to mix well with each other.

2. Add the chicken and coat well. Refrigerate for 1-2 hours to marinate.

3. Take Ninja Foodi Grill, arrange it over your kitchen platform, and open the top lid.

4. Arrange the grill grate and close the top lid.

5. Press "GRILL" and select the "MED" grill function. Adjust the timer to 14 minutes and then press "START/STOP." Ninja Foodi will start pre-heating.

6. Take the skewers, thread the chicken, red onion, and zucchini. Thread alternatively.

7. Ninja Foodi is preheated and ready to cook when it starts to beep. After you hear a beep, open the top lid.

8. Arrange the skewers over the grill grate.

9. Close the top lid and allow it to cook until the timer reads zero. Baste the kebabs with a marinating mixture in between. Cook until the food thermometer reaches 165°F.

10. Serve warm.

Nutrition Values (Per Serving)

Calories: 277, Fat: 15.5g, Saturated Fat: 2g, Trans Fat: 0g, Carbohydrates: 9.5g, Fiber: 2g, Sodium: 523mg, Protein: 25g

Classic BBQ Chicken Delight

Prepping time: 5-10 minutes

Cooking time: 12 minutes

Servings: 4

Ingredients:

- 1/3 cup spice seasoning
- ½ tablespoon Worcestershire sauce
- 1 teaspoon dried onion, chopped
- 1 tablespoon bourbon
- 1 tablespoon brown sugar
- ½ cup ketchup
- 1 pinch salt
- 2 teaspoons BBQ seasoning
- 6 chicken drumsticks

Directions:

1. Take your saucepan and add listed ingredients except for drumsticks, stir cook for 8-10 minutes
2. Keep it on the side and let them cool
3. Pre-heat your Ninja Foodi Grill to MED and set the timer to 12 minutes
4. Once the beep sound is heard, arrange your drumsticks over the grill grate and brush with remaining sauce
5. Cook for 6 minutes, flip with some more sauce and grill for 6 minutes more
6. Enjoy once done!

Nutrition Values (Per Serving)

Calories: 300, Fat: 8 g, Saturated Fat: 1 g, Carbohydrates: 10 g, Fiber: 1.5 g, Sodium: 319 mg, Protein: 12.5 g

Delicious Maple Glazed Chicken

Prepping time: 10 minutes

Cooking time: 15 minutes

Servings: 4

Ingredients

- 2 pounds chicken wings, bone-in
- 1 teaspoon black pepper, ground
- ¼ cup teriyaki sauce
- 1 cup maple syrup
- 1/3 cup soy sauce
- 3 garlic cloves, minced
- 2 teaspoons garlic powder
- 2 teaspoons onion powder

Directions

1. Take a mixing bowl, add garlic, soy sauce, black pepper, maple syrup, garlic powder, onion powder, and teriyaki sauce, combine well

2. Add the chicken wings and combine well to coat

3. Arrange the grill grate and close the lid

4. Pre-heat Ninja Foodi by pressing the "GRILL" option and setting it to "MED" and timer to 10 minutes

5. Let it pre-heat until you hear a beep

6. Arrange the chicken wings over the grill grate lock lid and cook for 5 minutes

7. Flip the chicken and close the lid, cook for 5 minutes more

8. Cook until it reaches 165 degrees F

9. Serve warm and enjoy!

Nutrition Values (Per Serving)

Calories: 543, Fat: 26 g, Saturated Fat: 6 g, Carbohydrates: 46 g, Fiber: 4 g, Sodium: 648 mg, Protein: 42 g

BBQ Chicken Drumlets

Prepping time: 5-10 minutes

Cooking time: 12 minutes

Servings: 5

Ingredients

- 1/3 cup spice seasoning
- ½ tablespoon Worcestershire sauce
- 1 teaspoon dried onion, chopped
- 1 tablespoon bourbon
- 1 tablespoon brown sugar
- ½ cup ketchup
- 1 pinch salt
- 2 teaspoons seasoned BBQ
- 6 chicken drumlets

Directions

1. Take a deep pan and add listed ingredients except for drumlets, stir the mixture well
2. Place it over medium heat, and stir cook for 8-10 minutes
3. Keep the mix on the side
4. Pre-heat your Ninja Foodi Grill to "MED" mode and set the timer to 12 minutes
5. Once you hear beep arrange the drumsticks over grill grate and brush half of your prepared sauce
6. Cook for 6 minutes, flip and brush more sauce, cook for 6 minutes more
7. Serve and enjoy once done with any remaining sauce
8. Enjoy!

Nutrition Values (Per Serving)

Calories: 342, Fat: 9 g, Saturated Fat: 1 g, Carbohydrates: 10 g, Fiber: 2 g, Sodium: 319 mg, Protein: 12 g

Baked Coconut Chicken

Prepping time: 10 minutes

Cooking time: 12 minutes

Servings: 4

Ingredients

- 2 large eggs
- 2 teaspoons garlic powder
- 1 teaspoon salt
- ½ teaspoon ground black pepper
- ¾ cup coconut aminos
- 1-pound chicken tenders
- Cooking spray as needed

Directions

1. Pre-heat Ninja Foodi by squeezing the "AIR CRISP" alternative and setting it to "400 Degrees F" and timer to 12 minutes

2. Take a large-sized baking sheet and spray it with cooking spray

3. Take a wide dish and add garlic powder, eggs, pepper, and salt

4. Whisk well until everything is combined

5. Add the almond meal and coconut and mix well

6. Take your chicken tenders and dip them in the egg followed by dipping in the coconut mix

7. Shake off any excess

8. Transfer them to your Ninja Foodi Grill and spray the tenders with a bit of oil.

9. Cook for 12-14 minutes until you have a nice golden-brown texture

10. Enjoy!

Nutrition Values (Per Serving)

Calories: 180, Fat: 1 g, Saturated Fat: 0 g, Carbohydrates: 3 g, Fiber: 1 g, Sodium: 214 mg, Protein: 0 g

Grilled Orange Chicken

Prepping time: 5-10 minutes

Cooking time: 10 minutes

Servings: 5-6

Ingredients

- 2 teaspoons ground coriander
- 1/2 teaspoon garlic salt
- 1/4 teaspoon ground black pepper
- 12 chicken wings
- 1 tablespoon canola oil

Sauce

- 1/4 cup butter, melted
- 3 tablespoons honey
- 1/2 cup orange juice
- 1/3 cup Sriracha chili sauce
- 2 tablespoons lime juice
- 1/4 cup chopped cilantro

Directions

1. Coat chicken with oil and season with the spices; refrigerate for 2 hours to marinate.

2. Combine all the sauce ingredients and set aside. Optionally, you can stir-cook the sauce mixture for 3-4 minutes in a saucepan.

3. Take Ninja Foodi Grill, organize it over your kitchen stage, and open the top cover.

4. Organize the barbecue mesh and close the top cover.

5. Click "GRILL" and choose the "MED" grill function. Adjust the timer to 10 minutes and afterward press "START/STOP." Ninja Foodi will begin pre-warming.

6. Ninja Foodi is preheated and prepared to cook when it begins to signal. After you hear a blare, open the top.

7. Organize chicken over the grill grate.

8. Close the top lid and cook for 5 minutes. Now open the top lid, flip the chicken.

9. Close the top lid and cook for 5 more minutes.

Nutrition Values (Per Serving)

Calories: 327, Fat: 14g, Saturated Fat: 3.5g, Trans Fat: 0g, Carbohydrates: 19g, Fiber: 1g, Sodium: 258mg, Protein: 25g

Basil and Garlic Chicken Legs

Prepping time: 10 minutes

Cooking time: 35 minutes

Servings: 4

Ingredients

- 4 chicken legs
- 4 teaspoons basil, dried
- 2 teaspoons garlic, minced
- 2 tablespoons olive oil
- 1 lemon, sliced
- Pinch of pepper and salt

Directions

1. Pre-heat Ninja Foodi by squeezing the "AIR CRISP" alternative and setting it to "350 Degrees F" and timer to 20 minutes
2. Coat chicken with oil using a brush and drizzle with rest of the ingredients
3. Transfer to Ninja Foodi Grill
4. Add lemon slices around the chicken legs
5. Close the grill
6. Cook for 20 minutes
7. Serve and enjoy!

Nutrition Values (Per Serving)

Calories: 240, Fat: 18 g, Saturated Fat: 4 g, Carbohydrates: 3 g, Fiber: 2 g, Sodium: 1253 mg

Orange Grilled Chicken Meal

Prepping time: 5-10 minutes

Cooking time: 15 minutes

Servings: 4

Ingredients:

- 12 chicken wings
- 2 tablespoons lime juice
- ¼ cup cilantro, chopped
- 2 teaspoons coriander, grounded
- 1 tablespoon canola oil
- 1/3 cup Sriracha chili sauce
- ¼ cup butter, melted
- 3 tablespoons honey
- ½ cup of orange juice
- ½ teaspoon garlic salt
- ¼ teaspoon ground black pepper

Directions:

1. Coat the chicken with oil, season with spices
2. Let it chill for 2 hours
3. Add listed ingredients and keep it on the side
4. Cook for 3-4 minutes in a saucepan
5. Pre-heat your Ninja Foodi by pressing the "GRILL" option and setting it to "MED."
6. Set your timer to 10 minutes
7. Let it pre-heat until it beeps
8. Arrange chicken over grill grate, cook for 5 minutes
9. Flip and let it cook for 5 minutes more
10. Serve with sauce on top
11. Serve and enjoy!

Nutrition Values (Per Serving)

Calories: 320, Fat: 14 g, Saturated Fat: 4 g, Carbohydrates: 19 g, Fiber: 1 g, Sodium: 258 mg, Protein: 25 g

Hot and Sassy BBQ Chicken

Prepping time: 5-10 minutes

Cooking time: 18 minutes

Servings: 4

Ingredients

- 2 tablespoons honey
- 1-pound chicken drumstick
- 1 tablespoon hot sauce
- 2 cups BBQ sauce
- Juice of 1 lime
- Pepper and salt as needed

Directions

1. Take a bowl and add BBQ sauce, lime juice, honey, pepper, salt, hot sauce, and mix well

2. Take another mixing bowl and add ½ cup sauce and chicken mix well and add remaining ingredients

3. Let it sit for 1 hour to marinate

4. Pre-heat Ninja Foodi by pressing the "GRILL" option and setting it to "MED" and timer to 18 minutes

5. Let it pre-heat until you hear a beep

6. Arrange chicken over grill grate, cook until the timer reaches zero and internal temperature reaches 165 degrees F

7. Serve and enjoy!

Nutrition Values (Per Serving)

Calories: 423, Fat: 13 g, Saturated Fat: 6 g, Carbohydrates: 47 g, Fiber: 4 g, Sodium: 698 mg, Protein: 22 g

Turkey Tomato Burgers

Prepping time: 5-10 minutes

Cooking time: 40 minutes

Servings: 6

Ingredients

- 2/3 cup sun-dried tomatoes, chopped
- 1/4 teaspoon salt
- 1/4 teaspoon pepper
- 1 large red onion, chopped
- 1 cup crumbled feta cheese
- 2 pounds lean ground turkey
- 6 burger buns of your choice, sliced in half

Directions

1. In a mixing bowl, add all the ingredients. Combine the ingredients to mix well with each other.

2. Prepare six patties from the mixture.

3. Take Ninja Foodi Grill, arrange it over your kitchen platform, and open the top lid.

4. Arrange the grill grate and close the top lid.

5. Press "GRILL" and select the "MED" grill function. Adjust the timer to 14 minutes and then press "START/STOP." Ninja Foodi will start pre-heating.

6. Ninja Foodi is preheated and ready to cook when it starts to beep. After you hear a beep, open the top lid.

7. Arrange the patties over the grill grate.

8. Close the top lid and cook for 7 minutes. Now open the top lid, flip the patties.

9. Close the top lid and cook for 7 more minutes.

10. Serve warm with ciabatta rolls. Add your choice of toppings: lettuce, tomato, cheese, ketchup, cheese, etc.

Nutrition Values (Per Serving)

Calories: 298, Fat: 16g, Saturated Fat: 2.5g, Trans Fat: 0g, Carbohydrates: 32g, Fiber: 4g, Sodium: 321mg, Protein: 27.5g

Juicy Beef, Lamb and Pork Recipes

Chipotle-Raspberry Pork Chops

Prepping time: 10 minutes

Cooking time: 10 minutes

Servings: 4

Ingredients

- 1/2 cup seedless raspberry preServings:
- 4 bone-in pork loin chops (7 ounces each)
- 1 chipotle pepper in adobo sauce, finely chopped
- 1/2 teaspoon salt

Directions

1. Preheat the grill for five minutes.

2. In a saucepan, cook and stir preServings: and chipotle pepper over medium heat until heated through. Reserve 1/4 cup for serving. Sprinkle pork with salt; brush with remaining raspberry sauce.

3. Lightly grease a grill or broiler pan rack. set the temperature to MAX, and set time to five minutes. Select the option START/STOP to begin preheating.

Nutrition Values (Per Serving)

Calories 309, Total Fat 9g, Total Carbs 27g, Protein 30g

Grilled Beef Burgers

Prepping time: 5-10 minutes

Cooking time: 10 minutes

Servings: 4

Ingredients

- 4 ounces cream cheese
- 4 slices bacon, cooked and crumbled
- 2 seeded jalapeño peppers, stemmed, and minced
- ½ cup shredded Cheddar cheese
- ½ teaspoon chili powder
- ¼ teaspoon paprika
- ¼ teaspoon ground black pepper
- 2 pounds ground beef
- 4 hamburger buns
- 4 slices pepper Jack cheese
- Optional - Lettuce, sliced tomato, and sliced red onion

Directions

1. In a mixing bowl, combine the peppers, Cheddar cheese, cream cheese, and bacon until well combined.
2. Prepare the ground beef into 8 patties. Add the cheese mixture onto four of the patties; arrange a second patty on top of each to prepare four burgers. Press gently.
3. In another bowl, combine the chili powder, paprika, and pepper. Sprinkle the mixture onto the sides of the burgers.
4. Take Ninja Foodi Grill, organize it over your kitchen stage, and open the top cover.
5. Organize the flame broil mesh and close the top cover.
6. Press "Flame broil" and select the "HIGH" barbecue work. Change the clock to 4 minutes and afterward press "START/STOP." Ninja Foodi will begin pre-warming.
7. Ninja Foodi is preheated and prepared to cook when it begins to blare. After you hear a blare, open the top. Arrange the burgers over the grill grate.
8. Close the top lid and allow it to cook until the timer reads zero. Cook for 3-4 more minutes, if needed.
9. Cook until the food thermometer reaches 145°F. Serve warm.
10. Serve warm with buns. Add your choice of toppings: pepper Jack cheese, lettuce, tomato, and red onion.

Nutrition Values (Per Serving)

Calories: 783, Fat: 38g, Saturated Fat: 16g, Trans Fat: 0g, Carbohydrates: 25g, Fiber: 3g, Sodium: 1259mg, Protein: 57.5g

Bourbon Pork Chops

Prepping time: 5-10 minutes

Cooking time: 20 minutes

Servings: 4

Ingredients

- 4 boneless pork chops
- Ocean salt and ground dark pepper to taste
- ¼ cup apple cider vinegar
- ¼ cup soy sauce
- 3 tablespoons Worcestershire sauce
- 2 cups ketchup
- ¾ cup bourbon
- 1 cup packed brown sugar
- ½ tablespoon dry mustard powder

Directions

1. Take Ninja Foodi Grill, orchestrate it over your kitchen stage, and open the top cover. Orchestrate the flame broil mesh and close the top cover.

2. Click "GRILL" and choose the "MED" grill function. Adjust the timer to 15 minutes and click "START/STOP."

3. Ninja Foodi is preheated and prepared to cook when it begins to signal. After you hear a signal, open the top.

4. Arrange the pork chops over the grill grate.

5. Close the top lid and cook for 8 minutes. Now open the top lid, flip the pork chops.

6. Close the top lid and cook for 8 more minutes. Check the pork chops for doneness, cook for 2 more minutes if required.

7. In a saucepan, heat the soy sauce, sugar, ketchup, bourbon, vinegar, Worcestershire sauce, and mustard powder; stir-cook until boils.

8. Reduce heat and simmer for 20 minutes to thicken the sauce.

9. Coat the pork chops with salt and ground black pepper. Serve warm with the prepared sauce.

Nutrition Values (Per Serving)

Calories: 346, Fat: 13.5g, Saturated Fat: 4g, Trans Fat: 0g, Carbohydrates: 27g, Fiber: 0.5g, Sodium: 1324mg, Protein: 27g

Beef and Blue Cheese Penne with Pesto

Prepping time: 10 minutes

Cooking time: 30 minutes

Servings: 4

Ingredients

- 5 ounces fresh baby spinach (about 6 cups), coarsely chopped
- 2 cups grape tomatoes, halved
- 2 cups uncooked whole wheat penne pasta
- 2 beef tenderloin steaks (6 ounces each)
- 1/4 teaspoon salt
- 1/4 teaspoon pepper
- 1/3 cup prepared pesto
- 1/4 cup chopped walnuts
- 1/4 cup crumbled Gorgonzola cheese

Directions

1. Cook pasta refer to the package directions.

2. Meanwhile, sprinkle steaks with salt and pepper. Grill the steaks while covered over medium heat or broil 4 in. From heat 5 to 7 minutes on each side or until meat reaches desired doneness (for medium-rare, the temperature should read 135°F; medium, 140°F; medium-well, 145°F).

3. Drain the pasta and transfer to a large bowl. Add spinach, tomatoes, pesto, and walnuts; toss to coat. Cut steak into thin slices. Serve pasta mixture with beef; sprinkle with cheese.

Nutrition Values (Per Serving)

Calories 534, Total Fat 22g, Total Carbs 49g, Total Protein 35g

Spinach Salad with Steak & Blueberries

Prepping time: 30 minutes

Cooking time: 30 minutes

Servings: 4

Ingredients

- 1 cup fresh blueberries, divided
- ½ cup chopped walnuts, toasted (see Tips)
- 1 teaspoon sugar
- ½ teaspoon salt, divided
- 3 tablespoons fruity vinegar, such as raspberry vinegar
- 1 tablespoon minced shallot
- 3 tablespoons walnut oil or canola oil
- 8 cups baby spinach
- 1 pound sirloin steak or strip steak (1-1¼ inches thick), trimmed
- ½ teaspoon freshly ground pepper
- ¼ cup crumbled feta cheese

Directions

1. Preheat the grill for eight minutes.

2. Pulse quarter cup blueberries, quarter cup walnuts, vinegar, shallots, ¼ teaspoon salt, and sugar in a food processor to form a paste. With the running motor, add oil until incorporated. Then transfer the dressing to a big bowl.

3. Sprinkle the steak with pepper and the left quarter with teaspoon salt.

4. Insert grill grate in the unit and close the hood. Select the option GRILL, set the temperature to MAX, and set time to six minutes. Select the option START/STOP to begin preheating.

5. Add the spinach to a bowl with the dressing and toss to coat. Divide the spinach among four plates. Slice the steak thinly, crosswise. Top spinach with the feta, steak, and remaining blueberries and walnuts.

Nutrition Values (Per Serving)

Calories 394, Total Fat 26g, Total Carbs 11g, Protein 29g

Steak Pineapple Mania

Prepping time: 5-10 minutes

Cooking time: 8 minutes

Servings: 4-5

Ingredients

- ½ medium pineapple, cored and diced
- 1 jalapeño pepper, seeded, stemmed, and diced
- 1 medium red onion, diced
- 4 (6-8-ounce) filet mignon steaks
- 1 tablespoon canola oil
- Sea salt and ground black pepper to taste
- 1 tablespoon lime juice
- ¼ cup chopped cilantro leaves
- Chili powder and ground coriander to taste

Directions

1. Rub the fillets with the oil evenly, then season with the salt and black pepper.
2. Take Ninja Foodi Grill, arrange it over your kitchen platform, and open the top lid.
3. Arrange the grill grate and close the top lid.
4. Press "GRILL" and select the "HIGH" grill function. Adjust the timer to 8 minutes and then press "START/STOP." Ninja Foodi will start preheating.
5. Ninja Foodi is preheated and ready to cook when it starts to beep. After you hear a beep, open the top lid.
6. Arrange the fillets over the grill grate. Close the top lid and cook for 4 minutes. Now open the top lid, flip the fillets.
7. Close the top lid and cook for 4 more minutes. Cook until the food thermometer reaches 125°F.
8. In a mixing bowl, add the pineapple, onion, and jalapeño. Combine well. Add the lime juice, cilantro, chili powder, and coriander. Combine again.
9. Serve the fillets warm with the pineapple mixture on top.

Nutrition Values (Per Serving)

Calories: 536, Fat: 22.5g, Saturated Fat: 7g, Trans Fat: 0g, Carbohydrates: 21g, Fiber: 4g, Sodium: 286mg, Protein: 58g

Grilled Pork Tenderloin Marinated in Spicy Soy Sauce

Prepping time: 20 minutes

Cooking time: 140 minutes

Servings: 6

Ingredients

- ¼ cup reduced-sodium soy sauce
- 1 tablespoon finely grated fresh ginger
- 2 tablespoons sugar
- 1 large garlic clove, peeled and finely grated or minced
- 1 fresh red Thai chile (see Note) or cayenne chile pepper, stemmed, seeded and minced
- 1 tablespoon toasted sesame oil
- 1½ pounds pork tenderloin, trimmed of fat and cut into 1-inch-thick medallions

Directions

1. Preheat the grill for eight minutes.

2. Whisk the soy sauce and sugar in a medium bowl until the sugar is dissolved. Stir in ginger, garlic, chili, and oil.

3. Place the pork in a plastic bag. Add the marinade and then seal the bag, squeezing out the air. Turn the bag for coating the medallions. Refrigerate for two hours, turning bag once to redistribute the marinade.

4. Insert grill grate in the unit and close the hood. Remove the pork. Select the option GRILL, set the temperature to MED, and set time to six minutes. Select the option START/STOP to begin preheating.

Nutrition Values (Per Serving)

Calories 127, Total Fat 3g, Total Carbs 1g, Protein 24g

Lettuce Cheese Steak

Prepping time: 5-10 minutes

Cooking time: 16 minutes

Servings: 5-6

Ingredients

- 4 (8-ounce) skirt steaks
- 6 cups romaine lettuce, chopped
- ¾ cup cherry tomatoes halved
- ¼ cup blue cheese, crumbled
- Ocean salt and Ground Black Pepper
- 2 avocados, peeled and sliced
- 1 cup croutons
- 1 cup blue cheese dressing

Directions

1. Coat steaks with black pepper and salt.

2. Take Ninja Foodi Grill, mastermind it over your kitchen stage, and open the top. Organize the barbecue mesh and close the top.

3. Click "GRILL" and choose the "HIGH" function. Change the clock to 8 minutes and afterward press "START/STOP." Ninja Foodi will begin pre-warming.

4. Ninja Foodi is preheated and prepared to cook when it begins to blare. After you hear a blare, open the top cover.

5. Fix finely the 2 steaks on the barbeque mesh.

6. Close the top cover and cook for 4 minutes. Presently open the top cover, flip the steaks.

7. Close the top cover and cook for 4 additional minutes. Cook until the food thermometer comes to 165°F. Cook for 3-4 more minutes if needed. Grill the remaining steaks.

8. In a mixing bowl, add the lettuce, tomatoes, blue cheese, and croutons. Combine the ingredients to mix well with each other.

9. Serve the steaks warm with the salad mixture, blue cheese dressing, and avocado slices on top.

Nutrition Values (Per Serving)

Calories: 576, Fat: 21g, Saturated Fat: 8.5g, Trans Fat: 0g, Carbohydrates: 23g, Fiber: 6.5g, Sodium: 957mg, Protein: 53.5g

Turmeric Pork Chops with Green Onion Rice

Prepping time: 15 minutes

Cooking time: 15 minutes

Servings: 4

Ingredients

- 4 (6-oz.) bone-in pork chops
- 1/2 teaspoon kosher salt, divided
- 1/2 teaspoon black pepper, divided
- 3 tablespoons olive oil, divided
- 1 large garlic clove, halved
- 1/2 teaspoon ground turmeric
- 1 tablespoon fish sauce
- 2 teaspoons oyster sauce
- 1 teaspoon tomato paste
- 1 bunch green onions
- 2 (8.8-oz.) packages precooked brown rice (such as Uncle Ben's)
- 1/4 cup fresh cilantro leaves
- 1 lime, cut into 4 wedges

Directions

1. Heat the grill for 8 minutes before use. Rub pork with cut sides of garlic; discard garlic. Sprinkle pork with turmeric, 1/4 teaspoon salt, and 1/4 teaspoon pepper. Combine 2 tablespoons oil, fish sauce, oyster sauce, and tomato paste. Brush both sides of pork with half of the oil mixture. Grill pork for 4 minutes on each side or until the desired degree of doneness. Transfer to a plate; brush both sides of pork with the remaining oil mixture. Keep warm.

2. Add onions to grill. Over medium-high; grill for 2 minutes. Coarsely chop onions.

3. Heat rice according to package directions. Combine green onions, rice, remaining one tablespoon oil, 1/4 teaspoon salt, and 1/4 teaspoon pepper. Serve rice with pork. Sprinkle with cilantro; serve with lime wedges.

Nutrition Values (Per Serving)

Calories 431, Total Fat 19g, Total Carbs 37g, Total Protein 28g

Avocado Salsa Steak

Prepping time: 5-10 minutes

Cooking time: 18 minutes

Servings: 4

Ingredients

- 1 cup cilantro leaves
- 2 ripe avocados, diced
- 2 cups salsa Verde
- 2 beef flank steak, diced
- 1/2 teaspoon salt
- 1/2 teaspoon pepper
- 2 medium tomatoes, seeded and diced

Directions

1. Rub the beef steak with salt and black pepper to season well.

2. Take Ninja Foodi Grill, orchestrate it over your kitchen stage, and open the top cover.

3. Orchestrate the flame broil mesh and close the top cover.

4. Press "Barbecue" and select the "MED" flame broil work. Alter the clock to 18 minutes and afterward press "START/STOP." Ninja Foodi will begin pre-warming.

5. Ninja Foodi is preheated and prepared to cook when it begins to signal. After you hear a blare, open the top. Arrange the diced steak over the grill grate.

6. Close the top lid and cook for 9 minutes. Now open the top lid, flip the diced steak.

7. Close the top lid and cook for 9 more minutes.

8. In a blender, blend the salsa and cilantro. Serve the grilled steak with the blended salsa, tomato, and avocado.

Nutrition Values (Per Serving)

Calories: 523, Fat: 31.5g, Saturated Fat: 9g, Trans Fat: 0g, Carbohydrates: 38.5g, Fiber: 2g, Sodium: 301mg, Protein: 41.5g

Minted Tomato, Onion & Glazed Tofu Kebabs

Prepping time: 15 minutes

Cooking time: 40 minutes

Servings: 4

Ingredients

- 1 14-ounce package extra-firm water-packed tofu, drained
- 1 tablespoon lime juice
- 16 fresh mint leaves
- 4 plum tomatoes, quartered and seeded
- 1 tablespoon reduced-sodium soy sauce
- 1 teaspoon minced fresh ginger
- 1 onion, peeled, quartered and separated into layers
- 2 jalapeño peppers, seeded and cut into ½-inch pieces
- ¼ cup kecap manis

Directions

1. Preheat the grill for eight minutes.

2. Cut the tofu in half horizontally, cutting two large slices about one inch thick. Take a kitchen towel and place it on the cutting board. Set the tofu on the towel. Put another clean folded towel over the tofu.

3. Put a flat and heavyweight thing like a skillet on top; Drain it for fifteen minutes; then remove the weight and cut the tofu into 1½-inch pieces.

4. Combine the lime juice, soy sauce, and ginger in a bowl. Add the tofu and toss it to coat. Cover it and marinate in the refrigerator for fifteen minutes.

5. Tuck in a mint leaf into every tomato quarter and thread them onto four or eight skewers alternately with onion, tofu, and jalapenos.

6. Insert grill grate in the unit and close the hood. Select the option GRILL, set the temperature to LOW, and set time to ten minutes. Select the option START/STOP to begin preheating.

Nutrition Values (Per Serving)

Calories 178, Total Fat 6g, Total Carbs 20g, Protein 11g

Sausage and Pepper Grinders

Prepping time: 15 minutes

Cooking time: 26 minutes

Servings: 6

Ingredients

- 2 bell peppers, cut in quarters, seeds and ribs removed
- Kosher salt, as desired
- Ground black pepper, as desired
- 1 white onion, peeled, sliced in 1-inch rings
- 2 tablespoons canola oil, divided
- 6 raw sausages (4 ounces each), like hot Italian or Bratwurst
- 6 hot dog buns
- Condiments, as desired

Directions

1. Preheat for eight minutes.

2. Insert grill grate in the unit and close the hood. Select the option GRILL, set the temperature to LOW, and set time to twenty-six minutes. Select the option START/STOP to begin preheating.

3. When the unit starts beeping to signal that it has preheated, place steaks on the grill grate. Close hood and cook for 12 minutes.

4. After twelve minutes, transfer the peppers and onions to a medium mixing bowl. Place the sausages on the grill grate; close the hood and cook for 6 minutes.

5. After six minutes, flip the sausages. Close the hood and cook for six extra minutes.

6. Meanwhile, gently tear up the grilled onions into individual rings and mix them well with the peppers.

7. After six minutes, remove the sausages from the grill grate. Place the buns, cut-side them down, over the grill grate. Close the hood and cook for 2 remaining minutes.

8. When cooking is done, spread any desired condiments on the buns, then place the sausages in buns. Top each liberally with onions peppers and serve.

Nutrition Values (Per Serving)

Calories 628, Total Fat 39.9g, Total Carbs 44g, Protein 23.2g

Korean Chili Pork

Prepping time: 5-10 minutes

Cooking time: 8 minutes

Servings: 4

Ingredients

- 2 pounds pork, cut into ⅛-inch slices
- 5 minced garlic cloves
- 3 tablespoons minced green onion
- 1 yellow onion, sliced
- ½ cup soy sauce
- ½ cup brown sugar
- 3 tablespoons Korean red chili paste or regular chili paste
- 2 tablespoons sesame seeds
- 3 teaspoons black pepper
- Red pepper flakes to taste

Directions

1. Take a zip-lock bag, add all the ingredients. Shake well and refrigerate for 6-8 hours to marinate.
2. Take Ninja Foodi Grill, orchestrate it over your kitchen stage, and open the top.
3. Mastermind the barbecue mesh and close the top cover.
4. Click "GRILL" and choose the "MED" grill function. flame broil work. Modify the clock to 8 minutes and afterward press "START/STOP." Ninja Foodi will begin to warm up.
5. Ninja Foodi is preheated and prepared to cook when it begins to signal. After you hear a signal, open the top.
6. Fix finely sliced pork on the barbeque mesh.
7. Cover and cook for 4 minutes. Then open the cover, switch the side of the pork.
8. Cover it and cook for another 4 minutes.
9. Serve warm with chopped lettuce, optional.

Nutrition Values (Per Serving)

Calories: 621, Fat: 31g, Saturated Fat: 12.5g, Trans Fat: 0g, Carbohydrates: 29g, Fiber: 3g, Sodium: 1428mg, Protein: 53g

Grilled Steak Salad with Tomatoes & Eggplant

Prepping time: 40 minutes

Cooking time: 40 minutes

Servings: 4

Ingredients

- 1 tablespoon dried oregano
- 1 pound flank steak, trimmed
- 1 small eggplant (about 1 pound), cut lengthwise into ½-inch-thick slices
- 4 tablespoons extra-virgin olive oil, divided
- 1 teaspoon salt, divided
- ¾ teaspoon freshly ground pepper, divided
- 2 sweet Italian peppers or 1 large bell pepper, cut into 2-inch-wide strips
- 2 large tomatoes, cut into wedges
- 1 small red onion, thinly sliced
- 1 small clove garlic, minced
- 3 tablespoons red-wine vinegar

Directions

1. Preheat the grill for eight minutes.

2. Cook the oregano in a small skillet on medium heat and keep stirring until it is toasted, which will be about two minutes. Transfer it to a bowl.

3. Cut the steak in half, lengthwise; season it with half teaspoon each salt and pepper. Brush the peppers and eggplant with one tablespoon oil.

4. Insert grill grate in the unit and close the hood. Select the option GRILL, set the temperature to LOW, and set time to thirty minutes. Select the option START/STOP to begin preheating.

5. Add the tomatoes, garlic, and onion to a bowl with the oregano. Drizzle them with vinegar and the remaining 3 tablespoons oil. Season them with the remaining half teaspoon salt and quarter teaspoon pepper; toss to combine. Chop the eggplant and peppers and cut the steak across the grain into thin slices; add to the bowl and toss to combine.

Nutrition Values (Per Serving)

Calories 365, Total Fat 21g, Total Carbs 17g, Protein 27g

Crispy Fish and Seafood Recipes

Perfect Spanish Garlic Shrimp

Prepping time: 5-10 minutes

Cooking time: 10 minutes

Servings: 3

Ingredients

- 1 lemon, cut into wedges
- ½ teaspoon red pepper flakes
- ½ teaspoon salt
- ½ cup olive oil
- 1 and ½ pound shrimp, shelled and deveined
- 2 garlic cloves, minced

Directions

1. Rinse the shrimp and pat dry with paper towels. Combine the shrimp, olive oil, garlic, salt, and red pepper flakes in a medium bowl.

2. Toss gently to combine. Cover with plastic wrap and then refrigerate for at least 30 minutes or up to 2 hours.

3. Insert the Grill Grate and close the hood.

4. Select GRILL, set temperature to HIGH, and set time to 8 minutes. Select START/STOP to begin pre-heating.

5. Grill the shrimp for about 3 minutes, until they are opaque and firm to the touch. Serve the shrimp immediately in 4 small bowls with the lemon wedges.

Nutrition Values (Per Serving)

Calories: 453, Fat: 42 g, Saturated Fat: 15 g, Carbohydrates: 4 g, Fiber: 2 g, Sodium: 644 mg, Protein: 16 g

Curried Shrimp & Potato Kebabs

Prepping time: 30 minutes

Cooking time: 30 minutes

Servings: 4

Ingredients

- 12 new or baby potatoes
- 3 cloves garlic, minced
- ¼ teaspoon salt
- 3 tablespoons canola oil
- 2 tablespoons chopped fresh cilantro
- 1 tablespoon curry powder
- 20 peeled and deveined raw shrimp, tails left on (20-25 per pound; see Tip)
- ½ cup nonfat plain yogurt
- 1 teaspoon lime juice

Directions

1. Preheat the grill for eight minutes.

2. Put potatoes in a container. Microwave on High until they get tender when pierced with a fork, three to three and a half minutes.

3. Meanwhile, mix oil, cilantro, garlic, curry powder, and salt in a big bowl. Reserve two tablespoons of the mixture in a bowl. Add shrimp and potatoes to a large bowl; toss it to coat. Thread the shrimp and potatoes onto 4 twelve-inch skewers.

4. Insert grill grate in the unit and close the hood. Select the option GRILL, set the temperature to LOW, and set time to five minutes. Select the option START/STOP to begin preheating.

5. Stir the yogurt and lime juice in a small bowl of the reserved sauce. Serve each kebab with 2 tablespoons sauce.

Nutrition Values (Per Serving)

Calories 244, Total Fat 12g, Total Carbs 15g, Protein 19g

Shrimp Po' Boy

Prepping time: 30 minutes

Cooking time: 30 minutes

Servings: 4

Ingredients

- 2 cups finely shredded red cabbage
- 2 tablespoons dill pickle relish
- 1 pound peeled and deveined raw shrimp, (51-60 per pound; see Shopping Tip)
- 4 teaspoons canola oil, divided
- 2 tablespoons reduced-fat mayonnaise
- 2 tablespoons nonfat plain yogurt
- 1 teaspoon chili powder
- ½ teaspoon paprika
- 4 tomato slices, halved
- ¼ cup thinly sliced red onion
- ¼ teaspoon freshly ground pepper
- 4 whole-wheat hot dog buns, or small sub rolls, split

Directions

1. Preheat the grill for eight minutes.

2. Combine the cabbage, mayonnaise relish, and yogurt in a medium bowl.

3. Toss the shrimp with two teaspoons oil, paprika, chili powder, and pepper in a medium bowl. Place the remaining two teaspoons oil in a bowl. Dip it in a pastry brush in the water, then in the oil, and then brush the insides of each bun.

4. Insert grill grate in the unit and close the hood. Select the option GRILL, set the temperature to LOW, and set time to five minutes. Select the option START/STOP to begin preheating.

5. For assembling the sandwiches, divide the tomato and onion among the buns. Spread about one-third cup of cabbage mixture down the middle of each and top with about ½ cup grilled shrimp.

Nutrition Values (Per Serving)

Calories 285, Total Fat 9g, Total Carbs 30g, Protein 21g

Grilled Shrimp Cocktail with Yellow Gazpacho Salsa

Prepping time: 40 minutes

Cooking time: 60 minutes

Servings: 4

Ingredients

- 4 medium yellow tomatoes, (1 pound), seeded and finely chopped
- 1 stalk celery, finely chopped
- ½ small red onion, finely chopped
- 1 yellow bell pepper, finely chopped
- 1 medium cucumber, peeled, seeded and finely chopped
- 1 tablespoon Worcestershire sauce
- ½ teaspoon freshly ground pepper
- 2 tablespoons minced fresh chives
- 2 tablespoons white-wine vinegar
- 2 tablespoons lemon juice
- ¼ teaspoon salt
- Several dashes hot sauce, to taste
- 1 pound raw shrimp, (21-25 per pound; see Note), peeled and deveined
- 2 cloves garlic, minced
- 2 tablespoons minced fresh thyme

Directions

1. Preheat the grill for eight minutes.

2. Mix the tomatoes, cucumber, celery, bell pepper, onion, vinegar, lemon juice, chives, Worcestershire sauce, salt and pepper, and hot sauce in a big bowl. Cover it and chill for at least twenty minutes or for a single day.

3. Mix the shrimp, garlic, and thyme in a medium bowl; cover it and refrigerate for twenty minutes.

4. Insert grill grates in the unit and close the hood. Select the option GRILL, set the temperature to LOW, and set time to 2 minutes per side. Select the option START/STOP to begin preheating. Serve the shrimp with salsa in martini glasses.

Nutrition Values (Per Serving)

Calories 154, Total Fat 2g, Total Carbs 12g, Protein 22g

Grilled Salmon Packets

Prepping time: 5 minutes

Cooking time: 15-20 minutes

Servings: 4

Ingredients

- 4 salmon steaks (6 ounces each)
- 1 teaspoon lemon-pepper seasoning
- 1 cup shredded carrots
- 1 teaspoon dried parsley flakes
- 1/2 cup julienned sweet yellow pepper
- 1/2 cup julienned green pepper
- 4 teaspoons lemon juice
- 1/2 teaspoon salt
- 1/4 teaspoon pepper

Directions

1. Preheat the grill for five minutes.

2. Sprinkle the salmon with a lemon-pepper. Place each of the salmon steaks on a double thickness of heavy-duty foil (about 12 in. square). Top with carrots and peppers. Sprinkle with remaining ingredients.

3. Fold foil around fish and seal them tightly. Then Grill, covered, over medium heat for 15-20 minutes or until fish flakes easily with a fork.

Nutrition Values (Per Serving)

Calories 280, Total Fat 16g, Total Carbs 5g, Protein 29g

Grilled Lemon-Garlic Salmon

Prepping time: 10 minutes

Cooking time: 15-20 minutes

Servings: 4

Ingredients

- 2 garlic cloves, minced
- 1/2 teaspoon minced fresh rosemary
- 2 teaspoons grated lemon zest
- 1/2 teaspoon salt
- 1/2 teaspoon pepper
- 4 salmon fillets (6 ounces each)

Directions

1. Take a small bowl, mix the first five ingredients, and rub over fillets. Let it stand for 15 minutes. Coat the grill with cooking oil.

2. Preheat the grill for 8 minutes before use. Place salmon on the grill with the skin side up. Grill while covered over medium heat or broil 4 in. From heat 4 minutes. Turn and grill 3 to 6 minutes longer or until fish just begins to flake easily with a fork.

Nutrition Values (Per Serving)

Calories 264, Total Fat 16g, Total Carbs 1g, Total Protein 29g

Apricot-Chile Glazed Salmon

Prepping time: 25 minutes

Cooking time: 25 minutes

Servings: 4

Ingredients

- 2 tablespoons New Mexico red chili powder
- 3 tablespoons apricot jam
- ½ teaspoon salt
- 1¼-1½ pounds center-cut wild salmon (see Tip), skinned

Directions

1. Preheat the grill for eight minutes.
2. Combine the salt and chili powder in a bowl. Rub them onto both sides of salmon.
3. Place the jam in a saucepan; heat it over medium heat, keep stirring it until melted.
4. Insert grill grate in the unit and close the hood.
5. Select the option GRILL, set the temperature to MED, and set time to ten minutes. Select the option START/STOP to begin preheating. Use a pastry brush, coat the top of the salmon with the jam. Close the grill; cook until the salmon easily flakes with a fork, 3 to 5 minutes more. To serve, cut into 4 portions.

Nutrition Values (Per Serving)

Calories 218, Total Fat 6g, Total Carbs 12g, Protein 29g

Grilled Salmon with Mustard & Herbs

Prepping time: 15 minutes

Cooking time: 40 minutes

Servings: 4

Ingredients

- 2 lemons, thinly sliced, plus 1 lemon cut into wedges for garnish
- 20-30 sprigs mixed fresh herbs, plus 2 tablespoons chopped, divided
- 1 tablespoon Dijon mustard
- 1 pound center-cut salmon, skinned
- 1 clove garlic
- ¼ teaspoon salt

Directions

1. Preheat the grill for eight minutes.

2. Lay the two nine-inch pieces of heavy-duty foil on top of one another and place it on a baking sheet. Arrange the lemon slices in two layers in the center of the foil. Spread the herb sprigs on the lemons. With the chef's knife, mash the garlic with salt and form a paste. Transfer it to a small dish and then stir in mustard and the remaining two tablespoons of chopped herbs. Spread the mixture on double sides of the salmon. Place the salmon on top of the herb sprigs.

3. Slide off the foil and salmon from the baking sheet onto the grill Insert grill grate in the unit and close the hood. Select the option GRILL, set the temperature to MAX, and set time to twenty-four minutes. Select the option START/STOP to begin preheating.

4. Divide the salmon into four portions and serve it with lemon wedges.

Nutrition Values (Per Serving)

Calories 132, Total Fat 4g, Total Carbs 1g, Protein 23g

Grilled Salmon Soft Tacos

Prepping time: 20 minutes

Cooking time: 20 minutes

Servings: 4

Ingredients

- 2 tablespoons extra-virgin olive oil
- 1 tablespoon ancho or New Mexico chile powder
- 4 4-ounce wild salmon fillets, about 1-inch thick, skin on
- 1 tablespoon fresh lime juice
- ¼ teaspoon kosher salt
- ⅛ teaspoon freshly ground pepper
- 8 6-inch corn or flour tortillas, warmed
- Cabbage Slaw, (recipe follows)
- Citrus Salsa, (recipe follows)
- Cilantro Crema, (recipe follows)

Directions

1. Preheat the grill for eight minutes.

2. Combine chili powder, oil, lime juice, salt, and pepper in a bowl. Rub the spice mixture over salmon. Insert grill grate in the unit and close the hood. Select the option GRILL, set the temperature to LOW, and set time to eight minutes. Select the option START/STOP to begin preheating. Cut each of the fillets lengthwise into two pieces and then remove the skin.

3. To serve, place two tortillas on each plate. Divide the fish, Citrus Salsa, Cabbage Slaw, and Cilantro Crema among the tortillas.

Nutrition Values (Per Serving)

Calories 570, Total Fat 30g, Total Carbs 44g, Protein 31g

Easy BBQ Roast Shrimp

Prepping time: 5-10 minutes

Cooking time:7 minutes

Servings: 2

Ingredients

- ½ pound shrimps, large
- 3 tablespoons chipotle in adobo sauce, minced
- ½ orange, juiced
- ¼ cup BBQ sauce
- ¼ teaspoon salt

Directions

1. Add listed ingredients into a mixing bowl
2. Mix them well
3. Keep it aside
4. Pre-heat Ninja Foodi by pressing the "ROAST" option and setting it to "400 Degrees F."
5. Set the timer to 7 minutes
6. Let it pre-heat until you hear a beep
7. Arrange shrimps over Grill Grate and lock lid
8. cook for 7 minutes
9. Serve and enjoy!

Nutrition Values (Per Serving)

Calories: 173, Fat: 2 g, Saturated Fat: 0.5 g, Carbohydrates: 21 g, Fiber: 2 g, Sodium: 1143 mg, Protein: 17 g

Paprika Grilled Shrimp

Prepping time: 5-10 minutes

Cooking time:6 minutes

Servings: 4

Ingredients

- 1-pound jumbo shrimps, peeled and deveined
- 2 tablespoons brown sugar
- 1 tablespoon paprika
- 1 tablespoon garlic powder
- 2 tablespoons olive oil
- 1 teaspoon garlic salt
- ½ teaspoon black pepper

Directions

1. Add listed ingredients into a mixing bowl
2. Mix them well
3. Let it chill and marinate for 30-60 minutes
4. Pre-heat Ninja Foodi by pressing the "GRILL" option and setting it to "MED."
5. Set the timer to 6 minutes
6. Let it pre-heat until you hear a beep
7. Arrange prepared shrimps over the grill grate
8. Lock lid and cook for 3 minutes
9. Then flip and cook for 3 minutes more
10. Serve and enjoy!

Nutrition Values (Per Serving)

Calories: 370, Fat: 27 g, Saturated Fat: 3 g, Carbohydrates: 23 g, Fiber: 8 g, Sodium: 182 mg, Protein: 6 g

Grilled Salmon with White Bean and Arugula Salad

Prepping time: 15 minutes

Cooking time: 10 minutes

Servings: 4

Ingredients

- 1/4 teaspoon grated lemon rind
- 3 tablespoons fresh lemon juice
- 1 tablespoon chopped capers, rinsed and drained
- 2 tablespoons olive oil
- 1/8 teaspoon ground red pepper
- 3/4 teaspoon kosher salt, divided
- 1/2 teaspoon minced fresh garlic
- 1 (15-ounce) can unsalted Great Northern beans, rinsed and drained
- 1/4 teaspoon freshly ground black pepper
- Cooking spray
- 4 (6-ounce) salmon fillets
- 4 cups loosely packed arugula
- 1/2 cup thinly sliced red onion

Directions

1. Mix together juice, oil, capers, rind, 1/2 teaspoon salt, garlic, and red pepper in a bowl.

2. Place beans in the bowl and drizzle with two tablespoons caper mixture.

3. Heat a grill for 8 minutes before use. Coat the grill with cooking oil. Coat the salmon with cooking oil and sprinkle with remaining 1/4 teaspoon salt along with black pepper. Add salmon to grill while skin side down. Grill for 6 minutes. Turn salmon over; grill for 1 minute or until done. Keep them warm.

4. Add arugula along with onions to the bowl with beans. Sprinkle with remaining caper mixture and toss. Divide salad among four plates; top each serving with one fillet. Serve immediately.

Nutrition Values (Per Serving)

Calories 379, Total Fat 15g, Total Carbs 21g, Total Protein 40g

Teriyaki-Marinated Salmon

Prepping time: 5 minutes

Cooking time: 8 minutes

Servings: 4

Ingredients

- 4 uncooked skinless salmon fillets (6 ounces each)
- 1 cup teriyaki marinade

Directions

1. Put the fish fillets and teriyaki sauce in a big resealable plastic bag. Move the fillets around to coat everywhere with sauce. Refrigerate it for one to twelve hours as per your need.

2. Insert the grill grate in the unit and close the hood. Select the option GRILL, set the temperature to MAX, and set the time to eight minutes. Press START/STOP to begin preheating.

3. When the unit signals that it has preheated, put fillets on the grill, gently press them to maximize the grill marks. Close the hood and cook it for six minutes. There isn't a need to flip the fish while cooking.

4. After six minutes, check the fillets if done; the internal temperature should come at least 140°F. If necessary, close the hood and continue to cook for 2 more minutes.

5. After cooking, serve the fillets immediately.

Nutrition Values (Per Serving)

Calories 261, Total Fat 10.6g, Total Carbs 8g, Protein 33.3g

Grilled Fish Tacos

Prepping time: 30 minutes

Cooking time: 50minutes

Servings: 6

Ingredients

- 4 teaspoons chili powder, preferably made with New Mexico or ancho chiles (see Note)
- 2 tablespoons lime juice
- 2 tablespoons extra-virgin olive oil
- 1 teaspoon ground cumin
- 1 teaspoon onion powder
- 1 teaspoon garlic powder
- 1 teaspoon salt
- ½ teaspoon freshly ground pepper
- 2 pounds mahi-mahi or Pacific halibut (see Note), ½- ¾ inch thick, skinned and cut into 4 portions
- ¼ cup reduced-fat sour cream
- ¼ cup low-fat mayonnaise
- 2 tablespoons chopped fresh cilantro
- 1 teaspoon lime zest
- Freshly ground pepper
- 3 cups finely shredded red or green cabbage
- 2 tablespoons lime juice
- 1 teaspoon sugar
- ⅛ teaspoon salt
- 12 corn tortillas, warmed

Directions

1. To prepare the fish: Combine lime juice, chili powder, oil, cumin, onion powder, salt and pepper, garlic powder in a bowl. Rub the adobo over all the fish. Let it stand 20 to 30 minutes for the fish to absorb the flavor.

2. To prepare the coleslaw: Add lime juice, sour cream, mayonnaise, cilantro, lime zest, salt and pepper, sugar, in a medium bowl; mix them until smooth and creamy. Add the cabbage and toss it to combine. Refrigerate until ready to use.

3. Preheat the grill for eight minutes before use.

4. Insert grill grate in the unit and close the hood. Select the option GRILL, set the temperature to LOW, and set time to fifteen minutes. Select the option START/STOP to begin preheating.

5. Transfer the fish to a plate and then separate it into large chunks.

6. Serve the tacos by passing the fish, tortillas, coleslaw and taco garnishes separately

Nutrition Values (Per Serving)

Calories 334, Total Fat 10g, Total Carbs 30g, Protein 31g

Vietnamese Mixed Grill

Prepping time: 45 minutes

Cooking time: 30 minutes

Servings: 4

Ingredients

- 1.5 lbs chicken breast
- 1-2 lbs flat iron or sirloin steak
- 1.5 lbs extra-large shrimp

Marinade Ingredients

- 2/3 cup grapeseed oil (or other high smoke point oil)
- 2/3 cup rice wine vinegar
- 3 tbsp brown sugar
- 4 tbsp fish sauce
- 4 tbsp oyster sauce
- 3 tbsp hoisin sauce
- 1 tbsp soy sauce
- 1 tbsp lemongrass, chopped (or 1 Tablespoon lemongrass paste found in the produce section)
- 1 tbsp Sambal Oelek or Asian chili paste
- 5 garlic cloves, chopped
- 2 tsp black pepper

Vietnamese Dipping Sauce Ingredients

- 1/4 cup fish sauce
- 2 tsp sugar
- 1/4 cup lime juice
- 1/3 cup water
- 3 cloves of garlic, minced
- 1/2 tsp chilis, finely sliced (Thai Bird, Serrano or Jalapeno)

Directions

1. Making the Marinade: Combine all the ingredients of marinade in a blender and process until smoothened. Whisk the ingredients in a medium bowl and then set it aside. This marinade will make 2 cups.

2. Marinating The Meats: Start to pour the marinade over chicken and steak (about 1/3 cup each). Marinate in the fridge for at least 2 hours or overnight. Marinate the shrimp for just 15-20 minutes before grilling.

3. Grilling The Meats On The Ninja: Remove the meats from the fridge and marinade, letting as much drip off as possible. Preheat Ninja Foodie Grill on high. Then using grape seed, avocado, or canola oil brush, the grill grates and grill the chicken for 14 minutes flipping it halfway through. The steak will take seven to nine minutes. Again, flip it half-way through. Finally, grill the shrimp for three minutes. You can flip it if you like. Remember to brush the grates before you add new meat.

4. Making The Vietnamese Dipping Sauce (Nuoc Cham): Blend all ingredients in a bowl good for dipping. Adjust the seasonings according to the taste. Add chili to taste.

Nutrition Values (Per Serving)

Calories 530, Total Fat 11.3g, Total Carbs 2g, Protein 105g

Ginger Salmon with Cucumber Lime Sauce

Prepping time: 30 minutes

Cooking time: 10 minutes

Servings: 10

Ingredients

- 1 tablespoon grated lime zest
- 4 teaspoons sugar
- 1/2 teaspoon salt
- 1/4 cup lime juice
- 2 tablespoons olive oil
- 2 tablespoons rice vinegar or white wine vinegar
- 1/2 teaspoon ground coriander
- 1/2 teaspoon freshly ground pepper
- 2 teaspoons minced fresh ginger root
- 2 garlic cloves, minced
- 2 medium cucumbers, peeled, seeded and chopped
- 1/3 cup chopped fresh cilantro
- 1 tablespoon finely chopped onion

Salmon

- 1 tablespoon olive oil
- 1/2 teaspoon salt
- 1/3 cup minced fresh ginger root
- 1 tablespoon lime juice
- 1/2 teaspoon freshly ground pepper
- 10 salmon fillets (6 ounces each)

Directions

1. Place the first 13 ingredients of the list in a blender. Cover and process until pureed.

2. In a bowl, combine ginger, oil, salt, lime juice, and pepper. Rub over flesh side of salmon fillets.

3. Lightly oil the grill. Place salmon on grill, skin side down. Grill while covered over medium-high heat 10-12 minutes or until fish just begins to flake easily with a fork. Serve with sauce.

Nutrition Values (Per Serving)

Calories 324, Total Fat 20g, Total Carbs 7g, Total Protein 29g

Crab & Shrimp Stuffed Sole

Prepping time: 25 minutes

Cooking time: 10-15 minutes

Servings: 4

Ingredients

- 2 tablespoons whipped cream cheese
- 2 teaspoons minced chives
- 1 garlic clove, minced
- 1 can (6 ounces) crabmeat, drained, flaked and cartilage removed
- 1/2 cup chopped cooked, peeled shrimp
- 1/4 cup soft bread crumbs
- 1/4 cup butter, melted, divided
- 1 teaspoon grated lemon zest
- 1-1/2 cups cherry tomatoes
- 2 tablespoons dry white wine or chicken broth
- 1 teaspoon minced fresh parsley
- 4 sole fillets (6 ounces each)
- 2 tablespoons lemon juice
- 1/2 teaspoon salt
- 1/2 teaspoon pepper

Directions

1. In a small bowl, put the crab, shrimp, bread crumbs, 2 tablespoons butter, cream cheese, chives, garlic, lemon zest, and parsley. Spoon about 1/4 cup of stuffing onto each fillet; roll up and secure with toothpicks.

2. Put each fillet on a double thickness of heavy-duty foil (about 18x12 in.). Mix up the tomatoes, wine, lemon juice, salt, pepper, and remaining butter; spoon over fillets. Fold foil around fish and seal tightly.

3. Preheat the grill for 8 minutes before grilling anything. Grill while covered over medium heat for 12-15 minutes or until fish flakes easily with a fork. Open the foil slowly and carefully to allow steam to escape.

Nutrition Values (Per Serving)

Calories 352, Total Fat 16g, Total Carbs 6g, Total Protein 46g

Healthy Vegetarian Recipes

Delicious Cajun Eggplant

Prepping time: 5-10 minutes

Cooking time: 12 minutes

Servings: 4

Ingredients

- ¼ cup olive oil
- 2 small eggplants, cut into slices
- 3 teaspoons Cajun seasoning
- 2 tablespoons lime juice

Directions

8. Coat eggplant slices with oil, lemon juice, and Cajun seasoning

9. Take your Ninja Foodi Grill and press "GRILL" and set to "MED" mode, set the timer to 10 minutes

10. Let it preheat

11. Arrange eggplants over grill grate, lock lid and cook for 5 minutes

12. Flip and cook for 5 minutes more

13. Serve and enjoy!

Nutritional Values (Per Serving)

Calories: 362, Fat: 11 g, Saturated Fat: 3 g, Carbohydrates: 16 g, Fiber: 1 g, Sodium: 694 mg, Protein: 8 g

Honey Carrot Dish

Prepping time: 15 minutes

Cooking time: 10 minutes

Servings: 4

Ingredients

- 6 carrots, cut lengthwise
- 1 tablespoon rosemary, chopped
- 1 tablespoon honey
- 2 tablespoons butter, melted
- 1 tablespoon parsley, chopped
- 1 teaspoon salt

Directions

1. Take your Ninja Foodi Grill, open the lid
2. Arrange grill grate and close top
3. Pre-heat Ninja Foodi by pressing the "GRILL" option and setting it to "MAX."
4. Then set the timer for 10 minutes
5. Allow it pre-heat until it sounds a beep
6. Arrange carrots over the grill grate
7. Take the remaining ingredients and spread them
8. Drizzle honey, lock lid and cook for 5 minutes
9. Then flip sausages and cook for 5 minutes more
10. Once done, serve and enjoy!

Nutritional Values (Per Serving)

Calories: 80, Fat: 4 g, Saturated Fat: 1 g, Carbohydrates: 10 g, Fiber: 3 g, Sodium: 186 mg, Protein: 0.5 g

Mushroom Tomato Roast

Prepping time: 10 minutes

Cooking time: 15 minutes

Servings: 4

Ingredients

- 2 cups cherry tomatoes
- 2 cups cremini, button, or other small mushrooms
- 1/4 cup of vinegar (Sherry) or 1/4 cup of red wine
- 2 garlic cloves, finely chopped
- 1/2 cup extra-virgin olive oil
- 3 tablespoons chopped thyme
- Pinch of crushed red pepper flakes
- 1 teaspoon kosher salt
- 1/2 teaspoon black pepper
- 6 scallions, cut crosswise into 2-inch pieces

Directions

1. Take a zip-lock bag, add black pepper, salt, red pepper flakes, thyme, vinegar, oil, and garlic. Add mushrooms, tomatoes, and scallions.

2. Shake well and refrigerate for 30-40 minutes to marinate.

3. Take Ninja Foodi Grill, orchestrate it over your kitchen stage, and open the top.

4. Press "Prepare" and alter the temperature to 400°F. Modify the clock to 12 minutes and afterward press "START/STOP." Ninja Foodi will begin preheating.

5. Ninja Foodi is preheated and prepared to cook when it begins to blare. After you hear a blare, open the top.

6. Arrange the mushroom mixture directly inside the pot.

7. Close the top lid and allow it to cook until the timer reads zero.

8. Serve warm.

Nutrition Values (Per Serving)

Calories: 253, Fat: 24g, Saturated Fat: 4g, Trans Fat: 0g, Carbohydrates: 7g, Fiber: 2g, Sodium: 546mg, Protein: 1g

Tomato Salsa

Prepping time: 5-10 minutes

Cooking time: 10 minutes

Servings: 4

Ingredients

- 1 red onion, peeled, cut in quarters
- 1 jalapeño pepper, cut in half, seeds removed
- 5 Roma tomatoes, cut in half lengthwise
- 1 tablespoon kosher salt
- 2 teaspoons ground black pepper
- 2 tablespoons canola oil
- 1 bunch cilantro, stems trimmed
- Juice and zest of 3 limes
- 3 cloves garlic, peeled
- 2 tablespoons ground cumin

Directions

1. In a blending bowl, join the onion, tomatoes, jalapeño pepper, salt, dark pepper, and canola oil.

2. Take Ninja Foodi Grill, mastermind it over your kitchen stage, and open the top. Mastermind the barbecue mesh and close the top cover.

3. Press "Barbecue" and select the "Maximum" flame broil work. Change the clock to 10 minutes and afterward press "START/STOP." Ninja Foodi will begin preheating.

4. Ninja Foodi is preheated and prepared to cook when it begins to blare. After you hear a signal, open the top cover.

5. Arrange the vegetables over the grill grate.

6. Close the top lid and cook for 5 minutes. Now open the top lid, flip the vegetables.

7. Close the top lid and cook for five more minutes.

8. Blend the mixture in a blender and serve as needed.

Nutrition Values (Per Serving)

Calories: 169, Fat: 9g, Saturated Fat: 2g, Trans Fat: 0g, Carbohydrates: 12g, Fiber: 3g, Sodium: 321mg, Protein: 2.5g

Buttery Spinach Meal

Prepping time: 10 minutes

Cooking time: 15 minutes

Servings: 4

Ingredients

- 2/3 cup Kalamata olives, halved and pitted
- 1 and ½ cups feta cheese, grated
- 4 tablespoons butter
- 2 pounds spinach, chopped and boiled
- Pepper and salt to taste
- 4 teaspoons lemon zest, grated

Directions

1. Take a mixing bowl and add spinach, butter, salt, pepper and mix well

2. Pre-heat Ninja Foodi by pressing the "AIR CRISP" option and setting it to "340 Degrees F" and timer to 15 minutes

3. Let it pre-heat until you hear a beep

4. Arrange a reversible trivet in the Grill Pan, arrange spinach mixture in a basket and place basket in the trivet

5. Let them roast until the timer runs out

6. Serve and enjoy!

Nutrition Values (Per Serving)

Calories: 250, Fat: 18 g, Saturated Fat: 6 g, Carbohydrates: 8 g, Fiber: 3 g, Sodium: 309 mg, Protein: 10 g

Italian Squash Meal

Prepping time: 5-10 minutes

Cooking time: 16 minutes

Servings: 4

Ingredients

- 1 medium butternut squash, peeled, seeded and cut into ½ inch slices
- 1 and ½ teaspoons oregano, dried
- 1 teaspoon dried thyme
- 1 tablespoon olive oil
- ½ teaspoon salt
- ¼ teaspoon black pepper

Directions

1. Add slices alongside other ingredients into a mixing bowl
2. Mix them well
3. Pre-heat your Ninja Foodi by pressing the "GRILL" option and setting it to "MED."
4. Set the timer to 16 minutes
5. Allow it to pre-heat until it beep
6. Arrange squash slices over the grill grate
7. Cook for 8 minutes
8. Flip and cook for 8 minutes more
9. Serve and enjoy!

Nutritional Values (Per Serving)

Calories: 238, Fat: 12 g, Saturated Fat: 2 g, Carbohydrates: 36 g, Fiber: 3 g, Sodium: 128 mg, Protein: 15 g

Cool Rosemary Potatoes

Prepping time: 10 minutes

Cooking time: 20 minutes

Servings: 4

Ingredients

- 2 pounds baby red potatoes, quartered
- ½ teaspoon parsley, dried
- ¼ teaspoon celery powder
- 2 tablespoons extra virgin olive oil
- ¼ cup onion flakes, dried
- ½ teaspoon garlic powder
- ½ teaspoon onion powder
- ½ teaspoon salt
- ¼ teaspoon freshly ground black pepper

Directions

1. Add all listed ingredients into a large bowl

2. Toss well and coat them well

3. Pre-heat your Ninja Foodi by pressing the "AIR CRISP" option and setting it to 390 Degrees F

4. Set the timer to 20 minutes

5. Allow it to pre-heat until it beeps

6. Once preheated, add potatoes to the cooking basket

7. Close the lid and cook for 10 minutes

8. Shake the basket and cook for 10 minutes more

9. Check the crispness if it is done or not

10. Cook for 5 minutes more if needed

11. Serve and enjoy!

Nutritional Values (Per Serving)

Calories: 232, Fat: 7 g, Saturated Fat: 1 g, Carbohydrates: 39 g, Fiber: 6 g, Sodium: 249 mg, Protein: 4 g

Blissful Simple Beans

Prepping time: 5 minutes

Cooking time: 10 minutes

Servings: 4

Ingredients

- 1-pound green beans, trimmed
- 1 lemon, juiced
- 2 tablespoons vegetable oil
- Flaky sea salt as needed
- Fresh ground black pepper as needed
- Pinch of red pepper flakes

Directions

1. Add green beans into a medium-sized bowl and
2. Pre-heat your Ninja Foodi by pressing the "GRILL" option and setting it to "MAX."
3. Set the timer to 10 minutes
4. Allow it to pre-heat until it beeps
5. Once preheated, transfer green beans to Grill Grate
6. Close the lid and let them grill for 8-10 minutes
7. Toss them from time to time until all sides are blustered well
8. Squeeze lemon juice over green beans and top with red pepper flakes
9. Season with salt and pepper
10. Serve and enjoy!

Nutritional Values (Per Serving)

Calories: 100, Fat: 7 g, Saturated Fat: 1 g, Carbohydrates: 10 g, Fiber: 4 g, Sodium: 30 mg, Protein: 2 g

Cheddar Cauliflower Meal

Prepping time: 5-10 minutes

Cooking time: 15 minutes

Servings: 2

Ingredients

- ½ teaspoon garlic powder
- ½ teaspoon paprika
- Ocean salt and ground dark pepper to taste
- 1 head cauliflower, stemmed and leaves removed
- 1 cup Cheddar cheese, shredded
- Ranch dressing, for garnish
- ¼ cup canola oil or vegetable oil
- 2 tablespoons chopped chives
- 4 slices bacon, cooked and crumbled

Directions

1. Cut the cauliflower into 2-inch pieces.

2. In a blending bowl, include the oil, garlic powder, and paprika. Season with salt and ground dark pepper; join well. Coat the florets with the blend.

3. Take Ninja Foodi Grill, mastermind it over your kitchen stage, and open the top cover.

4. Mastermind the flame broil mesh and close the top cover.

5. Press "Flame broil" and select the "Maximum" barbecue work. Change the clock to 15 minutes and afterward press "START/STOP." Ninja Foodi will begin preheating.

6. Ninja Foodi is preheated and prepared to cook when it begins to signal. After you hear a blare, open the top.

7. Organize the pieces over the flame broil grind.

8. Close the top lid and cook for 10 minutes. Now open the top lid, flip the pieces and top with the cheese.

9. Close the top lid and cook for 5 more minutes. Serve warm with the chives and ranch dressing on top.

Nutrition Values (Per Serving)

Calories: 534, Fat: 34g, Saturated Fat: 13g, Trans Fat: 0g, Carbohydrates: 14.5g, Fiber: 4g, Sodium: 1359mg, Protein: 31g

Delicious Broccoli and Arugula

Prepping time: 10 minutes

Cooking time: 12 minutes

Servings: 4

Ingredients

- Pepper as needed
- ½ teaspoon salt
- Red pepper flakes
- 2 tablespoons extra virgin olive oil
- 1 tablespoon canola oil
- ½ red onion, sliced
- 1 garlic cloves, minced
- 1 teaspoon Dijon mustard
- 1 teaspoon honey
- 1 tablespoon lemon juice
- 2 tablespoons parmesan cheese, grated
- 4 cups arugula, torn
- 2 heads broccoli, trimmed

Directions

1. Pre-heat your Ninja Foodi Grill to MAX and set the timer to 12 minutes

2. Take a large-sized bowl and add broccoli, sliced onion, and canola oil, toss the mixture well until coated

3. Once you hear the beep, it is pre-heated

4. Arrange your vegetables over the grill grate, let them grill for 8-12 minutes

5. Take a medium-sized bowl and whisk in lemon juice, olive oil, mustard, honey, garlic, red pepper flakes, pepper, and salt

6. Once done, add the prepared veggies and arugula in a bowl

7. Drizzle the prepared vinaigrette on top, sprinkle a bit of parmesan

8. Stir and mix

9. Enjoy!

Nutritional Values (Per Serving)

Calories: 168, Fat: 12 g, Saturated Fat: 3 g, Carbohydrates: 13 g, Fiber: 1 g, Sodium: 392 mg, Protein: 6 g

Broccoli and Arugula Salad

Prepping time: 10 minutes

Cooking time: 12 minutes

Servings: 4

Ingredients

- 2 heads broccoli, trimmed into florets
- 4 cups arugula, torn
- 2 tablespoons parmesan cheese, grated
- 1 tablespoon lemon juice
- 1 teaspoon honey
- 1 teaspoon Dijon mustard
- 1 garlic clove, minced
- ½ red onion, sliced
- 1 tablespoon canola oil
- 2 tablespoons extra-virgin olive oil
- Red pepper flakes
- ¼ teaspoon of sea salt
- Black pepper, freshly grounded

Directions

1. Supplement the flame broil mesh and close the hood

2. Pre-heat Ninja Foodi by pressing the "GRILL" option at and setting it to "MAX" and timer to 12 minutes

3. Take a large bowl and combine the broccoli, sliced onions, canola oil

4. Toss until coated

5. Once it pre-heat until you hear a beep

6. Arrange the vegetables over the grill grate, lock lid and cook for 8 to 12 minutes

7. Take a medium bowl and whisk together lemon juice, mustard, olive oil, honey, garlic, red pepper flakes, salt, and pepper

8. Once cooked, combine the roasted vegetables and arugula in a large serving bowl

9. Drizzle with the vinaigrette to taste and sprinkle with parmesan cheese

10. Serve and enjoy!

Nutrition Values (Per Serving)

Calories: 168, Fat: 12 g, Saturated Fat: 3 g, Carbohydrates: 13 g, Fiber: 1 g, Sodium: 392 mg, Protein: 6 g

Honey Dressed Asparagus

Prepping time: 5-10 minutes

Cooking time: 15 minutes

Servings: 4

Ingredients

- 2 pounds asparagus, trimmed
- 4 tablespoons tarragon, minced
- ¼ cup honey
- 2 tablespoons olive oil
- 1 teaspoon salt
- ½ teaspoon pepper

Directions

1. Add asparagus, oil, salt, honey, pepper, tarragon into your bow
2. Toss them well
3. Pre-heat your Ninja Foodi by pressing the "GRILL" option and setting it to "MED."
4. Set the timer to 8 minutes
5. Allow it pre-heat until it makes a beep sound
6. Arrange asparagus over grill grate and lock lid
7. Cook for 4 minutes
8. Then flip asparagus and cook for 4 minutes more
9. Serve and enjoy!

Nutritional Values (Per Serving)

Calories: 240, Fat: 15 g, Saturated Fat: 3 g, Carbohydrates: 31 g, Fiber: 1 g, Sodium: 103 mg, Protein: 7 g

Mustard Green Veggie Meal

Prepping time: 10 minutes

Cooking time: 30-40 minutes

Servings: 4

Ingredients

Vinaigrette

- 2 tablespoons Dijon mustard
- 1 teaspoon salt
- ¼ teaspoon black pepper
- ½ cup avocado oil

- ½ olive oil
- ½ cup red wine vinegar
- 2 tablespoons honey

Veggies

- 4 sweet onions, quartered
- 4 yellow squash, cut in half
- 4 red peppers, seeded and halved

- 4 zucchinis, halved
- 2 bunches green onions, trimmed

Directions

1. Take a small bowl and whisk mustard, pepper, honey, vinegar, and salt

2. Add oil to make a smooth mixture

3. Mastermind the flame broil mesh and close the top cover

4. Pre-heat Ninja Foodi by pressing the "GRILL" option and setting it to "MED" and timer to 10 minutes

5. Let it pre-heat until you hear a beep

6. Arrange the onion quarters over the grill grate, lock lid and cook for 5 minutes

7. Flip the peppers and cook for 5 minutes more

8. Grill the other vegetables in the same manner with 7 minutes each side for zucchini, pepper, and squash and 1 minute for onion

9. Prepare the vinaigrette by mixing all the ingredients under vinaigrette in a bowl

10. Serve the grilled veggies with vinaigrette on top

11. Enjoy!

Nutrition Values (Per Serving)

Calories: 326, Fat: 4.5 g, Saturated Fat: 1 g, Carbohydrates: 35 g, Fiber: 4 g, Sodium: 543 mg, Protein: 8 g

Hearty Spinach Olive

Prepping time: 5-10 minutes

Cooking time: 15 minutes

Servings: 3

Ingredients

- 2 pounds spinach, chopped and boiled
- 1 and ½ cups feta cheese, grated
- 4 tablespoons butter
- 2/3 cup Kalamata olives, halved and pitted
- 4 teaspoons lemon zest, grated
- Pepper and salt to taste

Directions

1. Add spinach, butter, salt, pepper into a mixing bowl
2. Mix them well
3. Pre-heat your Ninja Foodi by pressing the "AIR CRISP" option and setting it to 340 Degrees F
4. Set the timer to 15 minutes
5. Allow it to pre-heat until it beeps
6. Arrange a reversible trivet in the Grill Pan
7. Arrange spinach mixture in a basket and place basket in the trivet
8. Let them roast for 15 minutes
9. Serve and enjoy!

Nutritional Values (Per Serving)

Calories: 250, Fat: 18 g, Saturated Fat: 3 g, Carbohydrates: 8 g, Fiber: 4 g, Sodium: 339 mg, Protein: 10 g

Air Grilled Brussels

Prepping time: 5-10 minutes

Cooking time: 12 minutes

Servings: 4

Ingredients

- 6 slices bacon, chopped
- 1 pound brussels sprouts, halved
- 2 tablespoons olive oil, extra virgin
- 1 teaspoon salt
- ½ teaspoon black pepper, ground

Directions

1. Add Brussels, olive oil, salt, pepper, and bacon into a mixing bowl
2. Pre-heat Ninja Foodi by pressing the "AIR CRISP" option and setting it to "390 degrees F."
3. Set the timer to 12 minutes
4. Allow it to pre-heat until it beeps
5. Arrange Brussels over basket and lock lid
6. Cook for 6 minutes
7. Shake it and cook for 6 minutes more
8. Serve and enjoy!

Nutritional Values (Per Serving)

Calories: 279, Fat: 18 g, Saturated Fat: 4 g, Carbohydrates: 12 g, Fiber: 4 g, Sodium: 874 mg

Delicious Snacks Recipes

Oregano Squash Dish

Prepping time: 5-10 minutes

Cooking time: 16 minutes

Servings: 4

Ingredients

- 1 medium butternut squash, peeled, seeded, and cut into ½ inch slices
- 1 and ½ teaspoons oregano, dried
- 1 teaspoon thyme, dried
- 1 tablespoon olive oil
- ½ teaspoon salt
- ¼ teaspoon black pepper

Directions

1. Add slices alongside other ingredients into a mixing bowl
2. Mix them well
3. Pre-heat Ninja Foodi by pressing the "GRILL" option and setting it to "MED."
4. Set the timer to 16 minutes
5. Let it pre-heat until you hear a beep
6. Arrange squash slices over the grill grate
7. Cook for 8 minutes
8. Then flip and cook for 8 minutes more
9. Serve and enjoy!

Nutrition Values (Per Serving)

Calories: 238, Fat: 12 g, Saturated Fat: 2 g, Carbohydrates: 36 g, Fiber: 3 g, Sodium: 128 mg, Protein: 15 g

Well Prepped Yogurt Broccoli

Prepping time: 5-10 minutes

Cooking time: 10 minutes

Servings: 2

Ingredients

- 1 pound broccoli, cut into florets
- 2 tablespoons yogurt
- ¼ teaspoon turmeric powder
- 1 tablespoon chickpea flour
- ¼ teaspoon spice mix
- ½ teaspoon salt
- ½ teaspoon red chili powder

Directions

1. Wash the broccoli florets thoroughly
2. Add all ingredients except florets into a mixing bowl
3. Mix them well
4. Add florets to the mix
5. Let them sit in the fridge for 30 minutes
6. Take your Ninja Foodi Grill and open the lid
7. Arrange grill grate and close top
8. Pre-heat Ninja Foodi by pressing the "AIR CRISP" option and setting it to "390 Degrees F
9. Set the timer to 10 minutes
10. Let it pre-heat until you hear a beep
11. Arrange florets over the Grill Basket and lock the lid
12. Cook for 10 minutes
13. Serve and enjoy!

Nutrition Values (Per Serving)

Calories: 113, Fat: 2 g, Saturated Fat: 0 g, Carbohydrates: 12 g, Fiber: 4 g, Sodium: 124 mg, Protein: 07 g

Delicious Grilled Honey Fruit Salad

Prepping time: 5-10 minutes

Cooking time: 5 minutes

Servings: 4

Ingredients

- 1 tablespoon lime juice, freshly squeezed
- 6 tablespoons honey, divided
- 2 peaches, pitted and sliced
- 1 can (9 ounces) pineapple chunks, drained and juiced reserved
- ½ pound strawberries washed, hulled, and halved

Directions

1. Take a shallow mixing bowl, then add respectively soy sauce, balsamic vinegar, oil, maple syrup and whisk well

2. Then add broccoli and keep it aside

3. Press the "GRILL" of the Ninja Foodi Grill and set it to "MAX" mode with 10 minutes timer

4. Keep it in the preheating process

5. When you hear a beat, add broccoli over the grill grate

6. After then lock the lid and cook until the timer shows 0

7. Lastly, garnish the food with pepper flakes and sesame seeds

8. Enjoy!

Nutrition Values (Per Serving)

Calories: 141, Fat: 7 g, Carbohydrate: 14 g, Protein: 4 g, Sodium: 853 mg, Fiber: 4 g, Saturated Fat: 1 g

Lovely Seasonal Broccoli

Prepping time: 10 minutes

Cooking time: 10 minutes

Servings: 4

Ingredients

- ½ teaspoon salt
- ½ teaspoon red chili powder
- ¼ teaspoon spice mix
- 2 tablespoons yogurt
- 1 tablespoon chickpea flour
- ¼ teaspoon turmeric powder
- 1 pound broccoli, cut into florets

Directions

1. Take your florets and wash them thoroughly
2. Take a bowl and add listed ingredients, except the florets
3. Add broccoli and combine the mix well; let the mixture sit for 30 minutes
4. Pre-heat your Ninja Foodi to AIR CRISP mode at 390 degrees F and set the timer to 10 minutes
5. Once you hear a beep, add florets and crisp for 10 minutes
6. Serve and enjoy once done!

Nutrition Values (Per Serving)

Calories: 111, Fat: 2 g, Saturated Fat: 1 g, Carbohydrates: 12 g, Fiber: 1 g, Sodium: 024 mg, Protein: 7 g

Mammamia Banana Boats

Prepping time: 19 minutes

Cooking time: 6 minutes

Servings: 4

Ingredients

- ½ cup peanut butter chips
- ½ cup of chocolate chips
- 1 cup mini marshmallows
- 4 ripe bananas

Directions

1. With the peel, slice a banana lengthwise and remember that not to cut all the way through.

2. Onward, reveal the inside of the banana by using your hand

3. Press the "GRILL" option and set this in "MEDIUM" to pre-heat Ninja Foodi with a 6 minutes timer

4. Until you hear a beep, keep it in the pre-heat process

5. Put the banana over the Grill Grate and lock the lid, let it cook for 4-6 minutes until chocolate melts and bananas are toasted

6. Serve and Enjoy!

Nutrition Values (Per Serving)

Calories: 505, Fat: 18 g, Carbohydrates: 82 g, Protein: 10 g, Sodium: 166 mg, Fiber: 6 g, Saturated Fat: 4 g

Fully Grilled Sweet Honey Carrot

Prepping time: 10 minutes

Cooking time: 10 minutes

Servings: 6

Ingredients

- 1 teaspoon salt

- 1 tablespoon honey

- 1 tablespoon rosemary, chopped

- 1 tablespoon parsley, chopped

- 6 carrots, cut lengthwise

- 2 tablespoons butter, melted

Directions

1. Pre-heat your Ninja Foodi Grill to MAX, set a timer for 10 minutes

2. Once you hear the beep, arrange carrots over the grill grate

3. Spread remaining ingredients and drizzle honey

4. Lock lid and cook for 5 minutes, flip and cook for 5 minutes more

5. Serve and enjoy!

Nutrition Values (Per Serving)

Calories: 80, Fat: 4 g, Saturated Fat: 1 g, Carbohydrates: 10 g, Fiber: 3 g, Sodium: 186 mg, Protein: 0.5 g

Complete Italian Squash

Prepping time: 5-10 minutes

Cooking time: 16 minutes

Servings: 4

Ingredients

- ¼ teaspoon black pepper
- 1 and ½ teaspoons dried oregano
- 1 tablespoon olive oil
- ½ teaspoon salt
- 1 teaspoon dried thyme
- 1 medium butternut squash, peeled, seeded, and cut into ½ inch slices

Directions

1. Take a mixing bowl and add slices and other ingredients, mix well
2. Pre-heat your Ninja Foodi Grill to MED and set the timer to 16 minutes
3. Once you hear the beep, arrange squash slices over the grill grate
4. Cook for 8 minutes, flip and cook for 8 minutes
5. Serve and enjoy!

Nutrition Values (Per Serving)

Calories: 238, Fat: 12 g, Saturated Fat: 2 g, Carbohydrates: 36 g, Fiber: 3 g, Sodium: 128 mg, Protein: 15 g

Crispy Brussels

Prepping time: 5-10 minutes

Cooking time: 12 minutes

Servings: 4

Ingredients

- 1 pound brussels sprouts, halved

- 6 slices bacon, chopped

- 2 tablespoons olive oil, extra virgin

- 1 teaspoon salt

- ½ teaspoon ground black pepper

Directions

1. Add Brussels, bacon, olive oil, salt, and pepper into a mixing bowl

2. Pre-heat Ninja Foodi by pressing the "AIR CRISP" option and setting it to "390 degrees F."

3. Set the timer to 12 minutes

4. Let it pre-heat until you hear a beep

5. Arrange Brussels over basket and lock lid

6. Cook for 6 minutes

7. Shake it generously and cook for 6 minutes more

8. Serve and enjoy!

Nutrition Values (Per Serving)

Calories: 279, Fat: 18 g, Saturated Fat: 4 g, Carbohydrates: 12 g, Fiber: 4 g, Sodium: 874 mg, Protein: 14 g

Broccoli Maple Grill

Prepping time: 5-10 minutes

Cooking time: 10 minutes

Servings: 4

Ingredients

- 2 teaspoons maple syrup
- 4 tablespoon balsamic vinegar
- 2 tablespoon canola oil
- 4 tablespoons soy sauce
- 2 heads broccoli, cut into floret
- Pepper flakes and sesame seeds for garnish

Directions

1. Take a shallow mixing bowl, then add respectively soy sauce, balsamic vinegar, oil, maple syrup and whisk well

2. Then add broccoli and keep it aside

3. Press the "GRILL" of the Ninja Foodi Grill and set it to "MAX" mode with 10 minutes timer

4. Keep it in the preheating process

5. When you hear a beat, add broccoli over the grill grate

6. After then lock the lid and cook until the timer shows 0

7. Lastly, garnish the food with pepper flakes and sesame seeds

8. Enjoy!

Nutrition Values (Per Serving)

Calories: 141, Fat: 7 g, Carbohydrate: 14 g, Protein: 4 g, Sodium: 853 mg, Fiber: 4 g, Saturated Fat: 1 g

Creamed Potato Corns

Prepping time: 5-10 minutes

Cooking time: 30-40 minutes

Servings: 4

Ingredients

- 1 and ½ teaspoon garlic salt
- ½ cup sour cream
- 1 jalapeno pepper, seeded and minced
- 1 tablespoon lime juice
- 1 teaspoon ground cumin
- ½ cup milk
- 2 poblano pepper
- ¼ teaspoon cayenne pepper
- 2 sweet corn years
- 1 tablespoon cilantro, minced
- 3 tablespoons olive oil

Directions

1. Drain potatoes and rub them with oil
2. Pre-heat your Ninja Foodi Grill to MED, setting a timer for 10 minutes
3. Once you hear the beep, arrange poblano peppers over the grill grate
4. Let them cook for 5 minutes, flip and cook for 5 minutes more
5. Grill remaining veggies in the same way, giving 7 minutes to each side
6. Take a bowl and whisk in the remaining ingredients and prepare your vinaigrette
7. Peel grilled corn and chop them
8. Divide ears into small pieces and cut the potatoes
9. Serve grilled veggies with vinaigrette
10. Enjoy!

Nutrition Values (Per Serving)

Calories: 344, Fat: 5 g, Saturated Fat: 1 g, Carbohydrates: 51 g, Fiber: 3 g, Sodium: 600 mg, Protein: 5 g

Grilled Honey Carrots

Prepping time: 15 minutes

Cooking time: 10 minutes

Servings: 4

Ingredients

- 6 carrots, cut lengthwise
- 1 tablespoon rosemary, chopped
- 2 tablespoons melted butter
- 1 tablespoon parsley, chopped
- 1 tablespoon honey
- 1 teaspoon salt

Directions

1. Take your Ninja Foodi Grill and open the lid
2. Arrange grill grate and close top
3. Pre-heat Ninja Foodi by pressing the "GRILL" option and setting it to "MAX."
4. Set the timer to 10 minutes
5. Let it pre-heat until you hear a beep
6. Arrange carrots over grill grate and spread the remaining ingredients, and drizzle honey
7. Lock lid and cook for 5 minutes
8. Flip sausages and cook for 5 minutes more
9. Serve and enjoy!

Nutrition Values (Per Serving)

Calories: 80, Fat: 4 g, Saturated Fat: 1 g, Carbohydrates: 10 g, Fiber: 3 g, Sodium: 186 mg, Protein: 0.5 g

Honey-Licious Asparagus

Prepping time: 5-10 minutes

Cooking time:15 minutes

Servings: 4

Ingredients

- 2 pounds asparagus, trimmed
- 4 tablespoons tarragon, minced
- ¼ cup honey
- 2 tablespoons olive oil
- 1 teaspoon salt
- ½ teaspoon pepper

Directions

1. Add asparagus, oil, salt, honey, pepper, tarragon into a mixing bowl
2. Toss them well
3. Pre-heat Ninja Foodi by pressing the "GRILL" option and setting it to "MED."
4. Set the timer to 8 minutes
5. Let it pre-heat until you hear a beep
6. Arrange asparagus over grill grate and lock lid
7. Cook for 4 minutes
8. Flip the asparagus and cook for 4 minutes more
9. Serve and enjoy!

Nutrition Values (Per Serving)

Calories: 240, Fat: 15 g, Saturated Fat: 3 g, Carbohydrates: 31 g, Fiber: 1 g, Sodium: 103 mg, Protein: 7 g

Honey Touched Bratwurst

Prepping time: 5-10 minutes

Cooking time: 10 minutes

Servings: 4

Ingredients

- ¼ cup honey
- 1 teaspoon steak sauce
- 2 tablespoons mayonnaise
- 4 brat buns, split
- ¼ cup Dijon mustard
- 4 bratwurst links, uncooked

Directions

1. First, mix the mustard with steak sauce and mayonnaise in a bowl.

2. Prepare and pre-heat the Ninja Foodi Grill on a High-temperature setting.

3. Once it is pre-heated, open the lid and place the bratwurst on the Grill.

4. Cover the Ninja Foodi Grill's lid and Grill on the "Grilling Mode" for 10 minutes per side until their internal temperature reaches 320 degrees F.

5. Serve with buns and mustard sauce on top

Nutrition Values (Per Serving)

Calories: 225, Fat: 17 g, Saturated Fat: 5 g, Carbohydrates: 13 g, Fiber: 3 g, Sodium: 284 mg, Protein: 6 g

Surprised Desserts Recipes

Mozzarella Sticks and Grilled Eggplant

Prepping time: 10 minutes

Cooking time: 14 minutes

Servings: 4

Ingredients

- Salt as needed
- ½ pound buffalo mozzarella, sliced into ¼ inch thick
- 12 large basil leaves
- 2 heirloom tomatoes, sliced into ¼ inch thickness
- 2 tablespoon canola oil
- 1 eggplant, ¼ inch thick

Directions

1. Take a large bowl and add the eggplant, add oil and toss well until coated well

2. Pre-heat your Ninja Foodi to MAX and set the timer to 15 minutes

3. Once you hear the beeping sound, transfer the prepared eggplants to your Grill and cook for 8-12 minutes until the surface is charred

4. Top with cheese slice, tomato, and mozzarella

5. Cook for 2 minutes, letting the cheese melt

6. Remove from grill and place 2-3 basil leaves on top of half stack

7. Place remaining eggplant stack on top alongside basil

8. Season well with salt and rest of the basil

9. Enjoy!

Nutritional Values (Per Serving)

Calories: 0, Fat: 19 g, Saturated Fat: 19 g, Carbohydrates: 11 g, Fiber: 4 g, Sodium: 1555 mg, Protein: 32 g

Homely Zucchini Muffin

Prepping time: 5-10 minutes

Cooking time:7 minutes

Servings: 4

Ingredients

- 4 whole eggs
- 1 zucchini, grated
- 2 tablespoons almond flour
- ½ teaspoon salt
- 1 teaspoon butter

Directions

1. Add zucchini, salt, and almond flour into a mixing bowl
2. Mix them well
3. Grease muffin molds with butter
4. Add zucchini mixture to them
5. Arrange muffin tins in your Ninja Foodi Grill
6. Then close the lid and cook on "Air Crisp" mode for 7 minutes at 375 degrees F
7. Serve and enjoy!

Nutrition Values (Per Serving)

Calories: 94, Fat: 8 g, Saturated Fat: 1.5 g, Carbohydrates: 2 g, Fiber: 0.5 g, Sodium: 209 mg, Protein: 7 g

Lovely Rum Sundae

Prepping time: 10 minutes

Cooking time: 8 minutes

Servings: 4

Ingredients

- Vanilla ice cream for serving
- 1 pineapple, cored and sliced
- 1 teaspoon cinnamon, ground
- ½ cup brown sugar, packed
- ½ cup dark rum

Directions:

1. Take a large deep bowl and add sugar, cinnamon, and rum

2. Add the pineapple in the layer, dredge them properly and make sure that they are coated well

3. Pre-heat your Foodi in "GRILL" mode with "MAX" settings, setting the timer to 8 minutes

4. Once you hear the beep, strain any additional rum from the pineapple slices and transfer them to the grill rate of your appliance

5. Press them down and grill for 6- 8 minutes. Make sure to not overcrowd the grill grate, Cook in batches if needed

6. Top each of the ring with a scoop of your favorite ice cream, sprinkle a bit of cinnamon on top

7. Enjoy!

Nutrition Values (Per Serving)

Calories: 240, Fat: 4 g, Saturated Fat: 1 g, Carbohydrates: 43 g, Fiber: 8 g, Sodium: 85 mg, Protein: 2 g

The Healthy Granola Bites

Prepping time: 10 minutes

Cooking time: 15-20 minutes

Servings: 4

Ingredients

- Salt and pepper to taste
- 1 tablespoon coriander
- A handful of thyme, diced
- ¼ cup of coconut milk
- 3 handful of cooked vegetables, your choice
- 3 ounce plain granola

Directions

1. Pre-heat your Ninja Foodi to 352 degrees F in AIR CRISP mode, set a timer to 20 minutes

2. Take a bowl and add your cooked vegetables, granola

3. Use an immersion blender to blitz your granola until you have a nice breadcrumb-like consistency

4. Add coconut milk to the mix and mix until you have a nice firm texture

5. Use the mixture to make granola balls and transfer them to your Grill

6. Cook for 20 minutes

7. Serve and enjoy!

Nutritional Values (Per Serving)

Calories: 140, Fat: 10 g, Saturated Fat: 3 g, Carbohydrates: 14 g, Fiber: 4 g, Sodium: 215 mg, Protein: 2 g

Marshmallow Banana Boat

Prepping time: 19 minutes

Cooking time: 6 minutes

Servings: 4

Ingredients

- 4 ripe bananas
- 1 cup mini marshmallows
- ½ cup of chocolate chips
- ½ cup peanut butter chips

Directions

1. Slice a banana lengthwise, keeping its peel.

2. Use your hands to open banana peel like a book, revealing the inside of a banana.

3. Divide marshmallow, chocolate chips, peanut butter among bananas, stuffing them inside/

4. Preheat Ninja Foodie by pressing the "GRILL" option and setting it to "MEDIUM" and timer to 6 minutes let it preheat until you hear a beep.

5. Transfer banana to Grill Grate and lock lid, cook for 4-6 minutes until chocolate melts and bananas are toasted.

6. Serve and enjoy!

Nutrition Values (Per Serving)

Calories: 505, Fat: 18 g, Saturated Fat: 13 g, Carbohydrates: 82 g, Fiber: 6 g, Sodium: 103 mg, Protein: 10 g

Rummy Pineapple Sunday

Prepping time: 10 minutes

Cooking time: 8 minutes

Servings: 4

Ingredients

- ½ cup dark rum
- ½ cup packed brown sugar
- 1 pineapple cored and sliced
- Vanilla ice cream, for serving

Directions

1. Take a large-sized bowl and add rum, sugar, cinnamon.

2. Add pineapple slices, arrange them in the layer. Coat mixture then let them soak for 5 minutes, per side.

3. Preheat Ninja Foodie by pressing the "GRILL" option and setting it to "MAX" and timer to 8 minutes.

4. Let it preheat until you hear a beep.

5. Strain extra rum sauce from pineapple.

6. Transfer prepared fruit in grill grate in a single layer, press down fruit and lock lid.

7. Grill for 6-8 minutes without flipping, work in batches if needed.

8. Once done, remove and top each pineapple ring with a scoop of ice cream, sprinkle cinnamon and serve Enjoy!

Nutrition Values (Per Serving)

Calories: 240, Fat: 4 g, Saturated Fat: 2 g, Carbohydrates: 43 g, Fiber: 3 g, Sodium: 32 mg, Protein: 2 g

Veggie Packed Egg Muffin

Prepping time: 5-10 minutes

Cooking time:7 minutes

Servings: 4

Ingredients

- 4 whole eggs
- 2 tablespoons almond flour
- 1 teaspoon butter
- 1 zucchini, grated
- ½ teaspoon salt

Directions

1. Add almond flour, zucchini, salt into a mixing bowl
2. Mix them well
3. Grease muffin molds with butter
4. Adds zucchini mixture to them
5. Arrange muffin tins in your Ninja Foodi Grill and lock the lid
6. Cook on "Air Crisp" mode for 7 minutes at 375 degrees F
7. Serve and enjoy!

Nutrition Values (Per Serving)

Calories: 94, Fat: 8 g, Saturated Fat: 1.5 g, Carbohydrates: 2 g, Fiber: 0.5 g, Sodium: 209 mg, Protein: 7 g

Lovely Rum Sundae

Prepping time: 10 minutes

Cooking time: 8 minutes

Servings: 4

Ingredients

- Vanilla ice cream for serving
- 1 pineapple, cored and sliced
- 1 teaspoon cinnamon, ground
- ½ cup brown sugar, packed
- ½ cup dark rum

Directions

1. Take a large deep bowl and add sugar, cinnamon, and rum

2. Add the pineapple in the layer, dredge them properly and make sure that they are coated well

3. Pre-heat your Foodi in "GRILL" mode with "MAX" settings, setting the timer to 8 minutes

4. Once you hear the beep, strain any additional rum from the pineapple slices and transfer them to the grill rate of your appliance

5. Press them down and grill for 6- 8 minutes. Make sure to not overcrowd the grill grate, cook in batches if needed

6. Top each of the ring with a scoop of your favorite ice cream, sprinkle a bit of cinnamon on top

7. Enjoy!

Nutritional Values (Per Serving)

Calories: 240, Fat: 4 g, Saturated Fat: 1 g, Carbohydrates: 43 g, Fiber: 8 g, Sodium: 85 mg, Protein: 2 g

Eggplant and Tomato Meal

Prepping time: 10 minutes

Cooking time: 14 minutes

Servings: 4

Ingredients

- 1 eggplant, sliced and ¼ inch thick
- ½ pound buffalo mozzarella, sliced into ¼ inch thick
- 2 heirloom tomatoes, cut into ¼ inch thick
- 12 large basil leaves
- 2 tablespoons canola oil
- Salt to taste

Directions

1. Add eggplant, oil into a large-sized bowl
2. Toss them well
3. Pre-heat Ninja Foodi by pressing the "GRILL" option and setting it to "MAX."
4. Set the timer to 15 minutes
5. Let it pre-heat until you hear a beep
6. Transfer eggplants to Grill Plant and lock lid
7. Cook for 8-12 minutes
8. Once done, top eggplant with one slice of tomato and mozzarella
9. Lock lid and cook for 2 minutes more until cheese melts
10. Once done, remove eggplant from the Grill
11. Place 2-3 basil leaves on top of half stack
12. Place remaining eggplant stacks on top with basil
13. Season with salt and garnish with remaining basil
14. Serve and enjoy!

Nutrition Values (Per Serving)

Calories: 0, Fat: 19 g, Saturated Fat: 19 g, Carbohydrates: 11 g, Fiber: 4 g, Sodium: 1555 mg, Protein: 32 g

Great Mac and Cheese Bowl

Prepping time: 10 minutes

Cooking time: 10 minutes

Servings: 4

Ingredients

- 1 tablespoon parmesan cheese, grated
- Salt and pepper to taste
- 1 and ½ cup cheddar cheese, grated
- ½ cup warm milk
- ½ cup broccoli
- 1 cup elbow macaroni

Directions

1. Pre-heat your Ninja Foodi to 400 degrees F in AIR CRISP mode, set a timer to 10 minutes
2. Once you hear the beep, it is pre-heated
3. Take a pot and add water, bring the water to a boil
4. Add macaroni and veggies, boil for 10 minutes until cooked
5. Drain pasta and veggies, toss pasta and veggies with cheese and sauce
6. Season well with salt and pepper and transfer to Ninja Foodi
7. Sprinkle more cheese on top and cook for 15 minutes
8. Take it out and let it cool for 10 minutes
9. Serve and enjoy!

Nutritional Values (Per Serving)

Calories: 180, Fat: 11 g, Saturated Fat: 3 g, Carbohydrates: 14 g, Fiber: 3 g, Sodium: 287 mg, Protein: 6 g

Garlic Flavored Artichoke Meal

Prepping time: 10 minutes

Cooking time: 10 minutes

Servings: 4

Ingredients

- 2 large artichokes, trimmed and halved
- 3 garlic cloves, chopped
- ½ a lemon, juiced
- ½ cup canola oil
- Salt and pepper to taste

Directions

1. Select GRILL mode and set your Ninja Foodi Grill to "MAX."
2. Set the timer to 10 minutes
3. Let it pre-heat until you hear a beep
4. Add lemon juice, oil, garlic into a medium-sized bowl
5. Season with salt and pepper
6. Brush artichoke halves with lemon garlic mix
7. Once ready, transfer artichokes to Grill
8. Press them down to maximize grill mark
9. Grill for 8-10 minutes; make sure to blistered on all sides
10. Serve and enjoy!

Nutrition Values (Per Serving)

Calories: 285, Fat: 28 g, Saturated Fat: 8 g, Carbohydrates: 10 g, Fiber: 3 g, Sodium: 137 mg, Protein: 3 g

Cute Marshmallow and Banana Boats

Prepping time: 19 minutes

Cooking time: 6 minutes

Servings: 4

Ingredients

- 4 ripe bananas
- 1 cup mini marshmallows
- ½ cup of chocolate chips
- ½ cup peanut butter chips

Directions

1. Slice a banana lengthwise, keeping its peel. Ensure not to cut all the way through .

2. Use your hands to open banana peel like a book, revealing the inside of a banana.

3. Divide marshmallow, chocolate chips, peanut butter among bananas, stuffing them inside.

4. Pre-heat Ninja Foodi by pressing the "GRILL" option and setting it to "MEDIUM" and timer to 6 minutes.

5. let it pre-heat until you hear a beep.

6. Transfer banana to Grill Grate and lock lid, cook for 4-6 minutes until chocolate melts and bananas are toasted.

7. Serve and enjoy!

Nutrition Values (Per Serving)

Calories: 505, Fat: 18 g, Saturated Fat: 6 g, Carbohydrates: 82 g, Fiber: 6 g, Sodium: 103 mg, Protein: 10 g

Spice Lover's Cajun Eggplant

Prepping time: 5-10 minutes

Cooking time:12 minutes

Servings: 4

Ingredients

- 2 small eggplants, cut into slices
- 3 teaspoons Cajun seasoning
- ¼ cup olive oil
- 2 tablespoons lime juice

Directions

1. Coat eggplant slices with oil, lemon juice, and Cajun seasoning in a mixing bowl
2. Take your Ninja Foodi Grill and press "GRILL," and set to "MED" mode
3. Set the timer to 10 minutes
4. Let it pre-heat until you hear a beep
5. Arrange eggplants over grill grate and lock lid
6. Cook for 5 minutes
7. Flip and cook for 5 minutes more
8. Serve and enjoy!

Nutrition Values (Per Serving)

Calories: 362, Fat: 11 g, Saturated Fat: 3 g, Carbohydrates: 16 g, Fiber: 1 g, Sodium: 694 mg, Protein: 8 g

Chocolate Cheesecake

Prepping time: 15 minutes

Cooking time: 15 minutes

Servings: 4

Ingredients

- 2 cups cream cheese, softened
- 2 eggs
- 2 tablespoons cocoa powder
- 1 teaspoon pure vanilla extract
- ½ cup Swerve

Directions

1. Add in eggs, cocoa powder, vanilla extract, swerve, cream cheese in an immersion blender and blend until smooth.
2. Pour the mixture evenly into mason jars.
3. Put the mason jars in the insert of Ninja Foodi and close the lid.
4. Select "Bake/Roast" and bake for 15 minutes at 360 degrees F.
5. Refrigerate for at least 2 hours.
6. Serve and enjoy.

Nutrition Values (Per Serving)

Calories 244, Total Fat 24.8 g, Saturated Fat 15.6 g, Cholesterol 32 mg, Sodium 204 mg, Total Carbs 2.1 g, Fiber 0.1 g, Sugar 0.4 g, Protein 4 g

Lemon Mousse

Prepping time: 15 minutes

Cooking time: 12 minutes

Servings: 2

Ingredients

- 4-ounce cream cheese softened
- ½ cup heavy cream
- 1/8 cup fresh lemon juice
- ½ teaspoon lemon liquid stevia
- 2 pinches salt

Directions

1. Take a bowl and mix cream cheese, heavy cream, lemon juice, salt, and stevia.
2. Pour this mixture into the ramekins and transfer the ramekins in the pot of Ninja Foodi.
3. Select "Bake/Roast" and bake for 12 minutes at 350 degrees F.
4. Pour into the serving glasses and refrigerate for at least 3 hours.
5. Serve and enjoy.

Nutrition Values (Per Serving)

Calories 305, Total Fat 31 g, Saturated Fat 19.5 g, Cholesterol 103 mg, Sodium 299 mg, Total Carbs 2.7 g, Fiber 0.1 g, Sugar 0.5 g, Protein 5 g

Printed in Great Britain
by Amazon